LEARNING TO RELEASE FROM GRIEF AND LOSS

JERMILA SEALYS

Foreword by **Dr. Nadine Collins**

Printed in the United States of America

All Scriptures are from the NEW KING JAMES VERSION

LETTING THE PAIN OUT

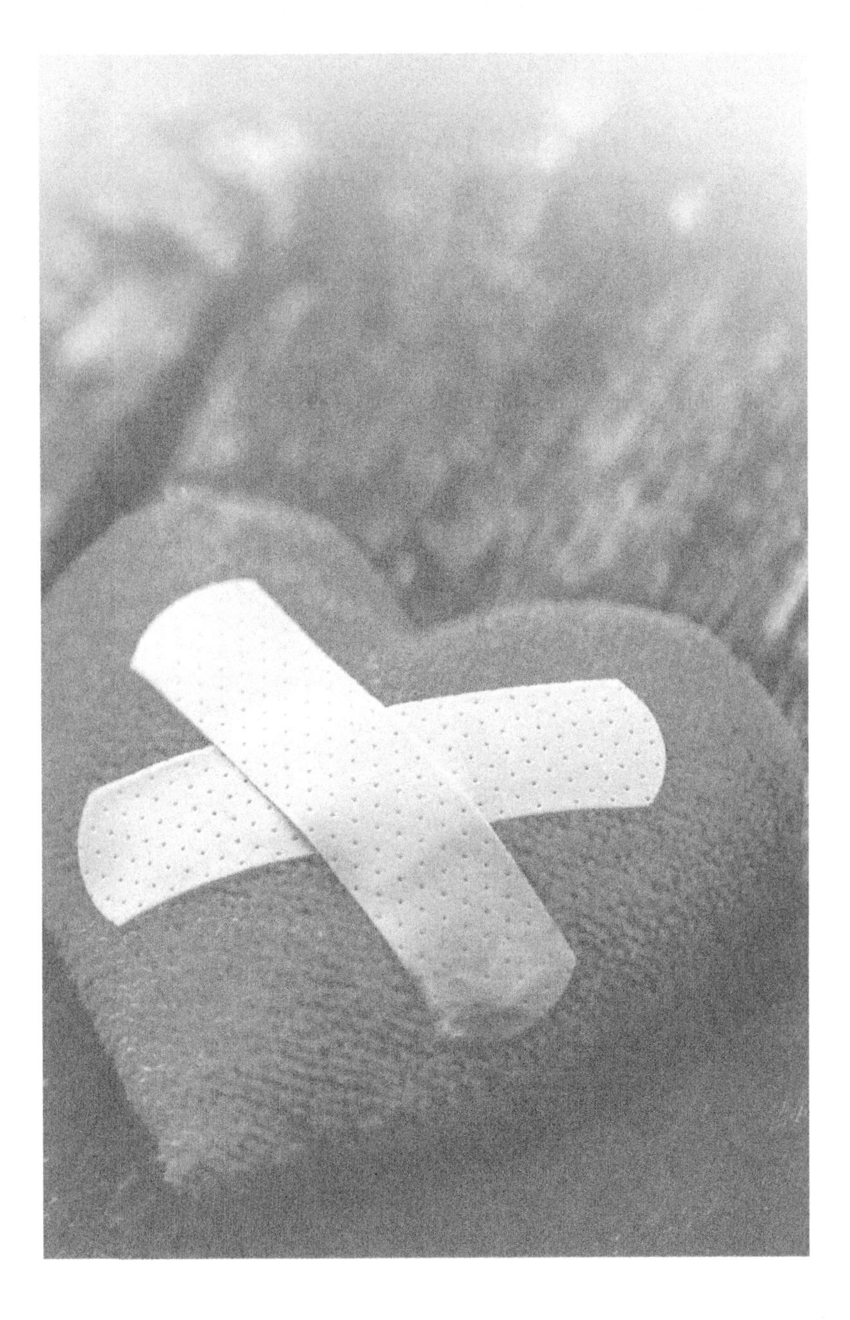

Contents

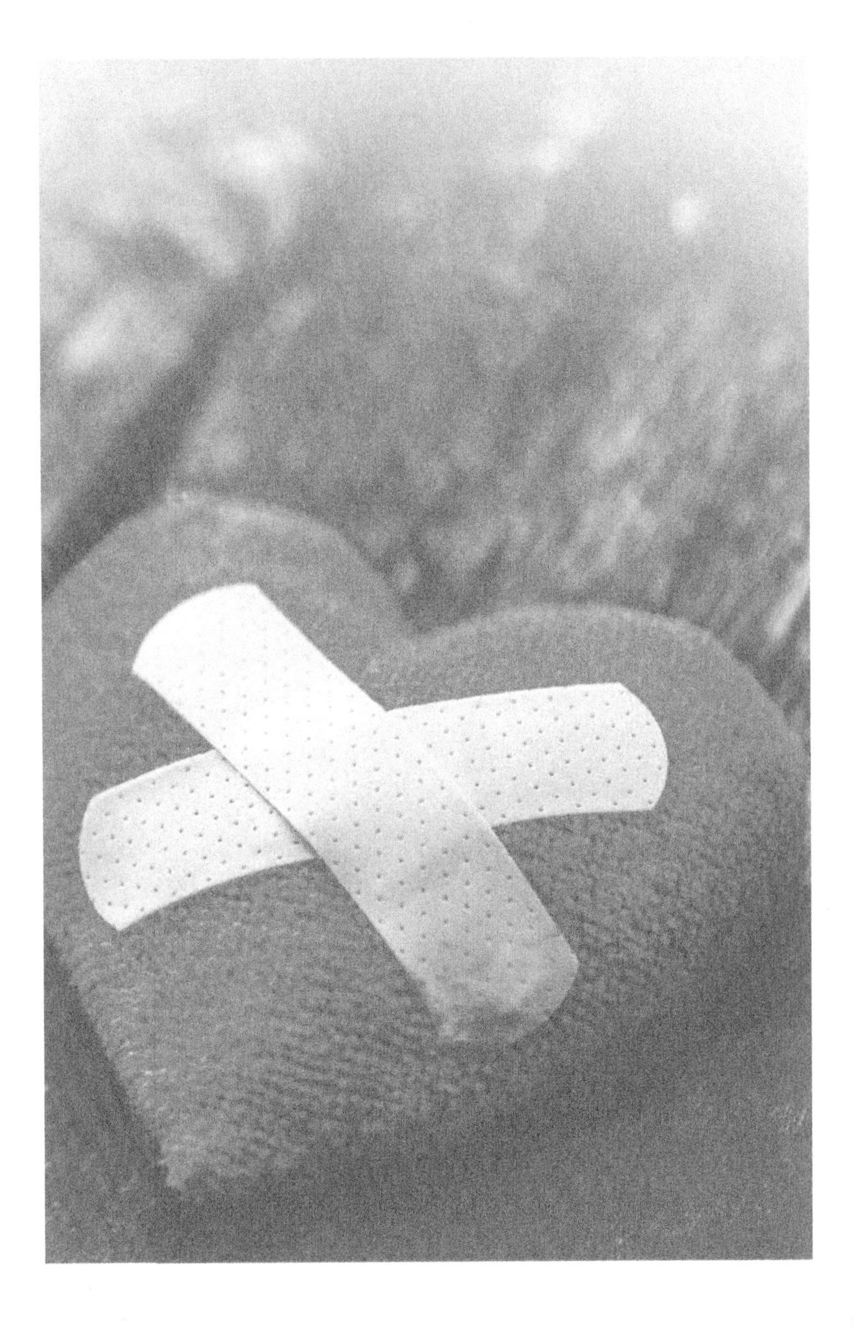

Dedication

In loving memory of my loved ones who passed away suddenly.

My mother, Rosalie Sealys, passed away in March 2020.

My sister, Curliana Sealys, passed away in June 2016.

My uncle and godfather, Stephen Joseph, passed away in May 2021.

My godmother, Agnes Celise, passed away in November 2020

My aunt, Marylin Octave nee Sealys, passed away in February 2017.

And to all my other family members and friends who have left this life.

Mom, life without you and Curliana is not easy.

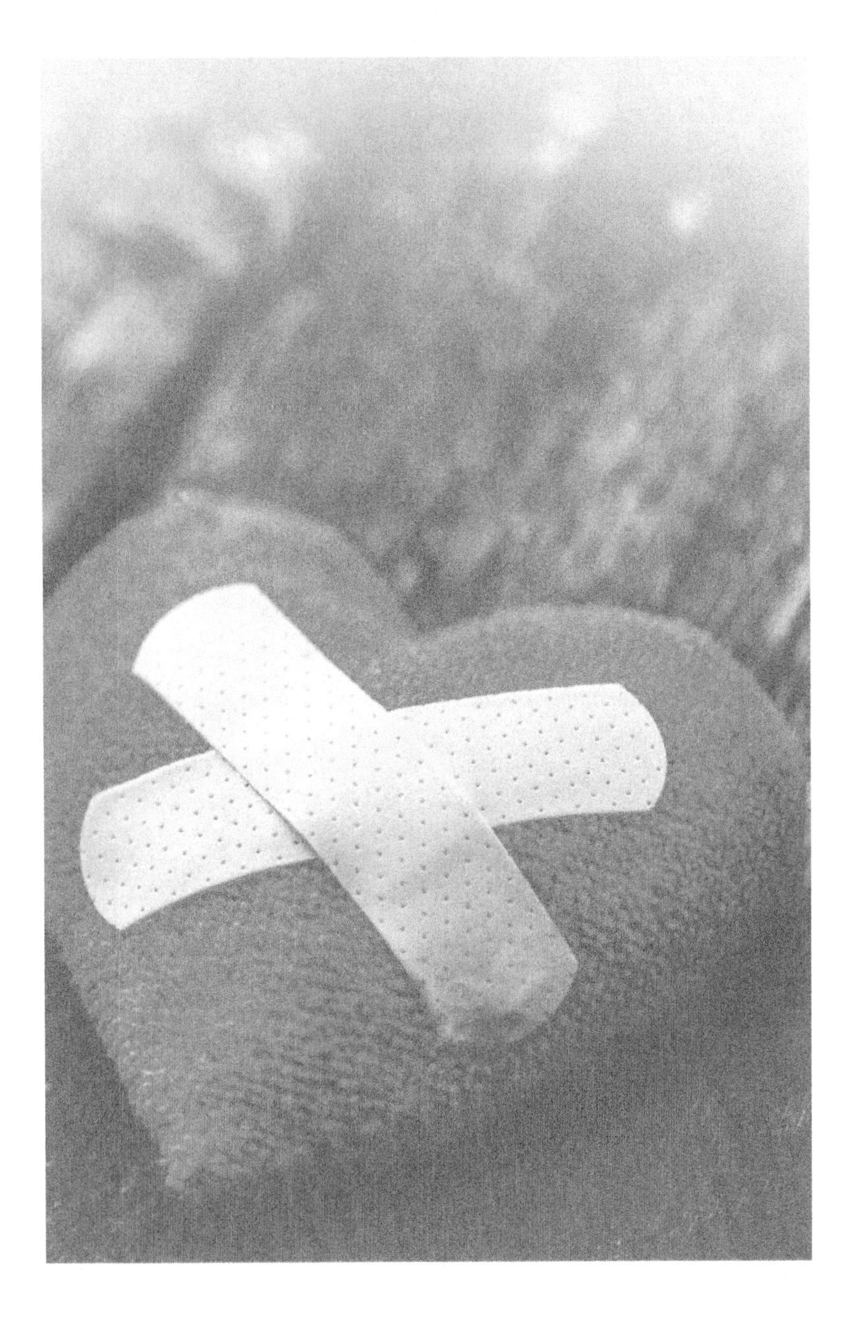

About the Book

'Letting the Pain Out' is me at my most vulnerable and powerless state. It reveals truths and lessons that I have endured during my over six years of silently battling grief at the sudden death and loss of loved ones. It is packed with stories of my struggle and how I finally managed grief without losing my mind. The silence and tireless tears that flooded the gates of my heart are finally now released. And as I share with you through the pages of this book, I continue to experience a form of healing and therapy.

We all go through grief and loss, no matter our ages, sex, race, or religion.

But it is from those same undesired experiences of the sudden deaths of my loved ones I am now positioned to do something I never thought possible. To write this book and help you find hope after the death of those you love.

This book will encourage and inspire you to embrace grief because death is a natural part of life. But more than that, it will help you navigate, cope, heal, and live in the presence of loss.

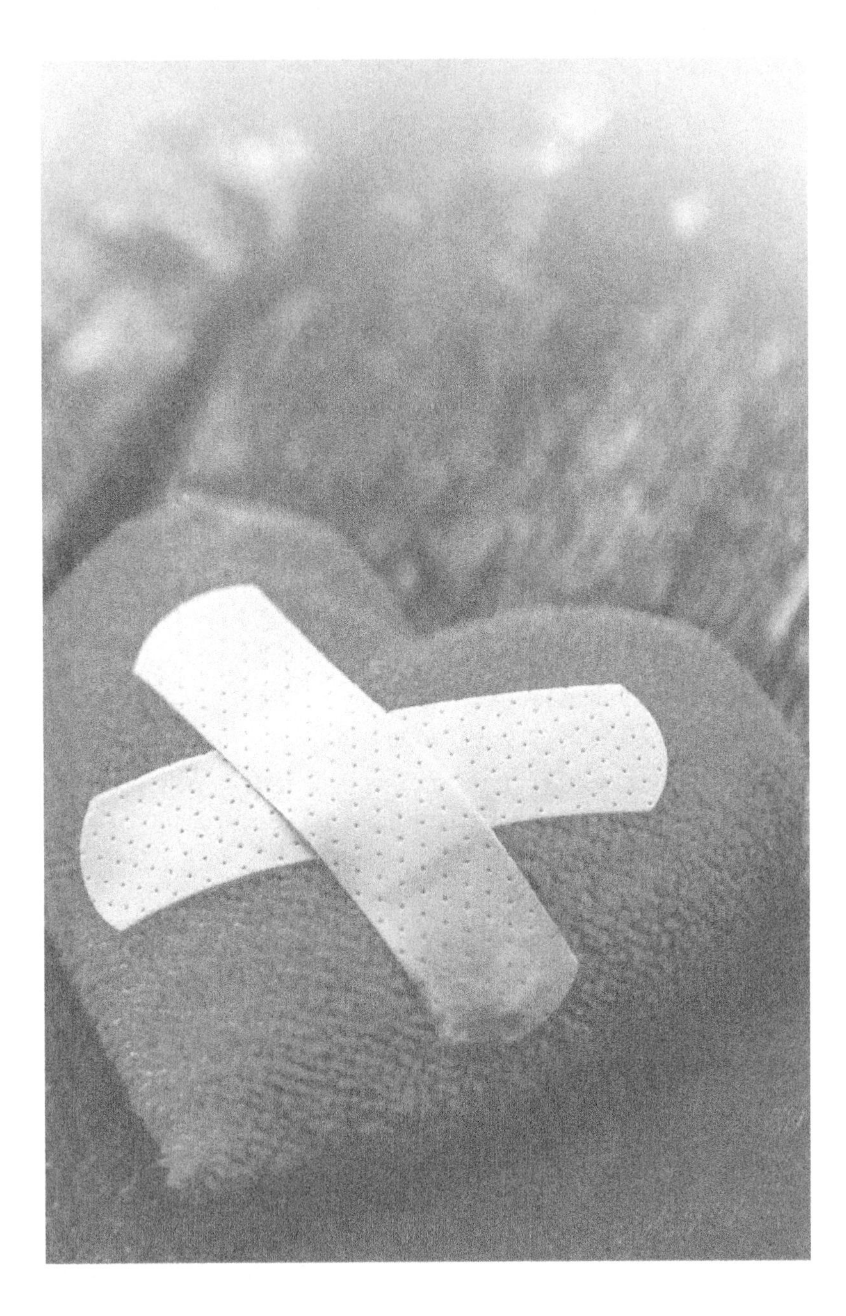

Foreword

I met Jermila on one of my trips to the United Kingdom where I was doing some training for a conference. We first bonded because we are from the same Caribbean island, but little did I know the long-reaching effects that one meeting would have.

Later, Jermila ordered my WOW Prayer book series online and kept in constant contact, giving me her feedback on what she read and how it was changing her life.

A few years later, Jermila attended my "Pregnant with Purpose Virtual Event," which is held in December every year to prepare women to be intentional about how they live in the coming year. It is at that virtual event Jermila felt there was a greater calling in her life.

A few days later, she reached out via email to share how the program had touched and affected her. She knew she was being called to do something greater, but she did not know what it was. A few months later, I got another email from her, in response to one of my campaign emails that was calling women to attend a free women's webinar if they wanted to become masterful speakers. At the end of the session, we invited women who were serious about becoming speakers to book a call with me. Jermila booked that Discovery Call with me, and right there in that 30-minute session decided it was her time to speak.

Note, Jermila is not someone who was out there doing public speaking. In fact, she was terrified of it. But she was committing to answering a call to do something that made her uncomfortable, something that terrified her to the core. She did it because she believed deep down, she had something to share, even though she was not exactly sure what that was, and how she would develop the confidence to put herself "out there."

So, she enrolled in the twelve to fourteen weeks Speaker Mentorship Group Program. During that program, Jermila revealed her story of how many close loved ones she had lost through death in a short period. In her own reserved and quiet way, she shared how deeply hurt she felt as people made insensitive comments about these losses, linking it to possible family curses. She knew other people in the world were probably hurting as much as she was. They too were hiding their pain of loss because they were afraid of being judged.

It was during that program Jermila intentionally began her journey to deeper healing. One of her tasks or assignments was to build her signature story. That is when the pain began to come out. According to her, the more she wrote, the more she healed. So, she kept writing until that story, an abridged version of her painful experiences, was finished.

But Jermila was not finished. She felt that sharing her story through her speaking platform was liberating, but many more people needed to address the topic of death, loss, and grief. She wanted to have a greater impact by helping others to "talk," to begin openly conversing about this topic that is so taboo within certain religious and cultural circles. She felt called to do it, so she signed up for the Elite Book Coaching Experience.

As you read this book, think of it as a memoir of sorts that will help you to release the pain in you that was created by any loss. You may have grieved in silence for many years because, like Jermila, you wanted to be strong for everybody else but you. Like her, you may have suffered behind the scenes because you felt others had expiration dates on how long and how much you should grieve.

Like Jermila, you are probably afraid others are looking at you and your family and making judgments about why you lost so much. So you bottled everything inside.

But this book gives you the permission to finally release and let the pain out. It is your literal moment to breathe deeply and let it all out without shame.

Jermila writes to you from the darkest and most painful experiences of her life but also a place of peace, love, and compassion. Her every word is almost written with a smile as she shares experiences and lessons that will help you to cry, scream, raise your hands, and release as you feel liberated to let the pain out so that you grieve in peace and heal openly.

Dr. Nadine Collins

Women's Leadership & Empowerment Coach,

International Speaker,

Author of the WOW Prayer Book Series

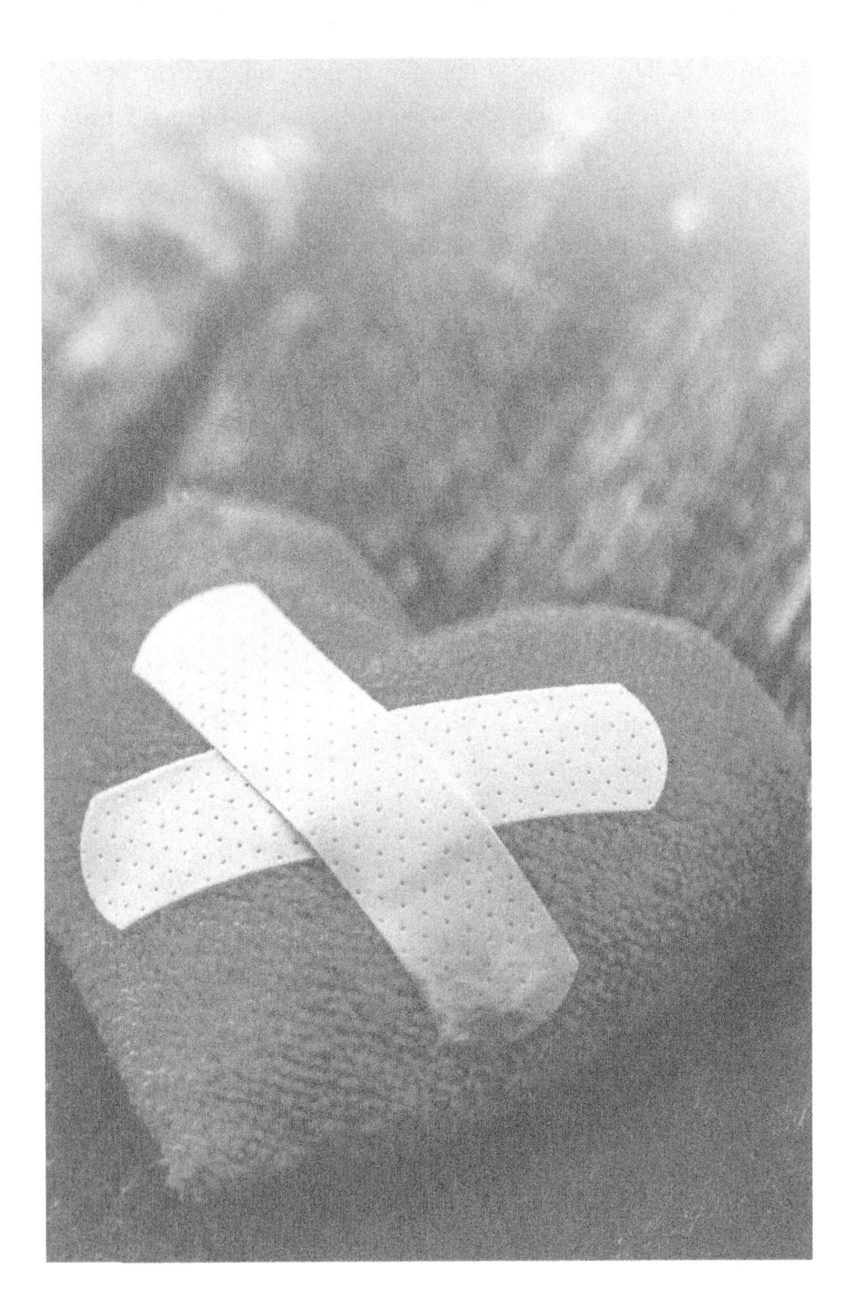

Prologue

I am Jermila Sealys, the firstborn of five children to my beautiful and phenomenal mother Rosalie Sealys. I grew up on the beautiful Caribbean island of St. Lucia with my four siblings: one brother and three sisters.

Life was a bit challenging at times in a single-parent household, but my mother always worked and tried to support us as best as she could.

At the tender age of 17, I became a mother of a beautiful baby girl named Latisha. It was a joyous day when I lay eyes on her.

As life continued, I realized I needed to pursue a better life and future for my family and young daughter. Hence, my mom decided to take parental responsibility for her.

Collectively as a family, we agreed I would migrate to the United Kingdom, with my mom's help and blessing, to commence my military training at 18 years old.

After a few years of service in the Army, I enrolled in university to complete my degree in nursing. Life was good, and I was happy.

We were happy. We celebrated many achievements along the way: my sister's graduation, the birth of my nieces and nephews, birthdays, and other joyous occasions.

I traveled back and forth to St. Lucia to spend time with my family, and we made the best of life as we could. However, we did not have much. My life was better than any fairy tale I could have imagined—happily ever after. There were tears, but they were not the painful ones. They were more often tears of joy.

On June 8, 2016, I received a call that had a major impact on my life until this day. Sometimes, I wish I had never answered that call. I wasn't prepared to accept what I heard in the fateful wee hours of the morning. I crashed to the ground on my knees and hands.

Gradually, I curled up on the spot and as I took the call, I screamed with a force that could not have been contained within the tiny walls of my stomach. As the pressure from the pit of my stomach traveled to my vocal cords, it exploded, followed by the involuntary movement of my body in a cat pose position, punching at the carpet beneath.

The jolt of the news I had just received sent shock waves through my body, and my brain could not decode the message. Instantaneously, my body responded with a cold, yet, hot wave of sweat and uncontrolled tremors.

For once, I was speechless and lost for words. My vocabulary had failed me momentarily.

I could not understand at that moment why my colleagues were watching me in utter silence. Their unspoken words were translated in their eyes as if to say, "Hurry up! We can't wait in suspense any longer." I knew they could tell it wasn't good news, but they patiently waited for me to be comfortable enough to relay the message.

I wanted to feel her warm embrace and rest my head on her chest where she could assure me it would be okay. All I had was her voice, the same voice that had delivered this devastating news. Within her voice, I could feel her pain. It was no longer sweet and warm, but instead, there was a touch of coldness.

Many mixed emotions saturated my head, posing endless questions. How could this have happened to my family?

You were so young. You still have all your dreams and hopes for your life—places to go, things to do, and most importantly, your children to raise—all taken away from you without warning, without a sign.

It's been too long since I have failed to show up because I am crippled by the pain your loss caused. This grip you placed on me has kept me imprisoned by the walls of my thoughts.

I feel powerless against the knee you place on my neck, crushing my windpipe beneath. I long to escape. I long to speak, but the words would not leave my lips and my voice could not be heard—too numb, too sore, and too afraid to fight back.

We battle day and night as you bruise my ego. I'm so afraid to sleep at night because I am not sure what your next step is. I should be able to handle you. After all, I am a soldier and a nurse with a solid Christian faith. I am a hero in other people's eyes—but defenseless against you.

Come with me on my journey with grief as I explain how I was bruised and battered for the past six years by the sudden death of my sister, mother, aunties, uncles, grandmother, and cousin.

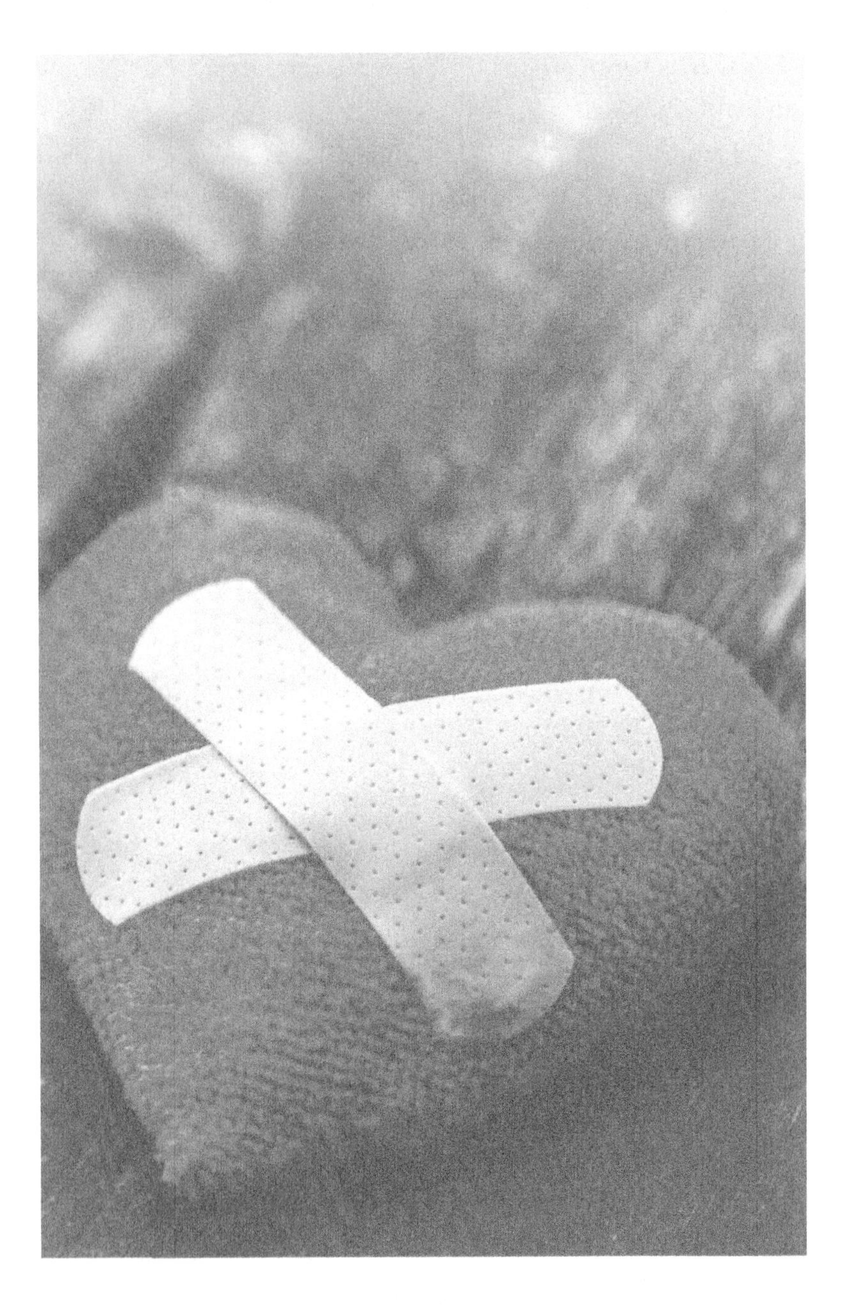

CHAPTER 1

Picture in a Frame

"A picture is worth a thousand words."
—FRED R.BARNAR

As I look at the glass silver frame on the brown-stained mahogany stand in the corner of my living room, it brings back memories of our very last family outing together. On that day, you wore your yellow and blue sundress, had your hair neatly plaited in cornrow, and stylishly carried your long umbrella in your hand.

It was the 39th independence celebration of my birth land St. Lucia. Our family went on a beautiful outing at a private beach on an islet near the Vieux fort harbor.

It was a lovely, sunny day with crystal blue skies. It was the perfect day to go to the beach or any other outdoor activity. I could feel the warmth of the sun as it penetrated my brown tan skin as sweat made its way to the surface.

Breaking the silence of the morning, the birds chirped; dogs barked, and the familiar voices of friends and family in the neighborhood could be heard as they greeted each other. Then, as usual, my uncle Max turned up the volume of the radio that was tuned into the local station. There was no need for us to put our radio on as all the songs and news were well received from the ones that were already on.

As I stepped outside, I realized the morning dew had dried up on the neatly cut green grass. I could feel the cool morning breeze on my skin and face. The weather was looking promising, and we could go ahead with our plans for the day.

As it was a national holiday, we decided to spend the day at the beach and have a cookout. My cousin slept over so we could start our day on time.

The kids were excited at the news that we were going to spend the day at the beach and were up before anyone could rouse them. Usually, on any other day, someone would have to do the honors of waking them up.

"Aunty, are we going to the beach today? It's not raining. Remember you said if there isn't any rain we would spend the day at the beach."

"Yes, I know," I said.

Without even waiting for an explanation from me, my nieces, Abney and Angel, had already changed into their swimwear. They were too excited to even sit still for just a brief second. Amid the excitement, they decided to wait for us on the balcony while we got things in order for our outing.

The youngest member of the family with us that day was Jerbarry, my sister's son. He was just four months old at the time.

My mother and I packed all the ingredients and utensils we needed for the cookout, including the pots, pans, and bowls. Mother and my cousin had already cleaned and seasoned the meat and fish the night before. My sister, daughter, and cousins got the individual stuff ready to take with them for the day. However, before we left home, we had our breakfast that my mother had already prepared.

After eating, we were all set to leave our homes for the adventure ahead. As we were about to drive off, my cousin Zack met us by the vehicle and decided he wanted to come along with his sister and brother. So we had to wait an extra twenty minutes for them to get their bag with a change of clothes. That's how Amy and Kurtell became part of the family fun.

The drive to the jetty took about fifteen minutes, and then we traveled to the islet on a family fishing boat. When we got to the jetty, we took a few pictures before putting our stuff into the boat and making the short journey. The seawater was crystal clear with small waves crashing against the wall.

The ride across was smooth as the boat rode every wave with caution. The kids were excited and looked out for sea creatures in the water. "I see one," they shouted every time they saw something.

We made it across and secured the boat while we offloaded. With everyone off the fishing boat, we looked for a secure place to store our belongings, though we were the only ones on the beach at the time. The water was warm and inviting, clear closer to the shore and aqua blue further out.

The kids did not waste any time. Immediately, they were in the water playing and bathing, which is what they spent most of the day doing anyway. They found their spot and started building sandcastles and rolling in the sand. It was a nightmare getting the sand out of the girls' hair the following day.

At first, my mom was reluctant for my sister to come on the excursion as she had only given birth to my nephew four months prior. But my sister did not want this moment to pass her by, so she insisted she come along. Little did we know that four months later, she would no longer be with us—just the picture in the frame. This image reminds me of a day full of love and fun, a day painted vividly and beautifully in my mind. It awakens a part of me that will never be taken away.

My sister took out her beach blanket and three or four of our towels and spread them on the sand. Then she placed two baby blankets and carefully positioned her sleeping infant under the shade of the trees nearby.

Sitting next to her baby, she took in the sight of us playing and having fun in the water, smiling every time my eyes made contact with her. She looked happy and relaxed. My sister wasn't a woman of many words, but her smile would cut the silence.

My mother strategically positioned three stones, collected some wood nearby, and set up a fire with a pot of water so she could cook to feed her troop.

She made our favorite one-pot meal: chicken backs, lentils, and dumplings, Lucians' favorite fast food. We also had a grill covered with a few pot fish and barbeque wings, and the smell was heavenly.

The day went by swiftly. It was already dark and late evening when we got home. But not without its share of trouble. Halfway on our journey back home, our vehicle broke down and could not take us home. As it was a holiday, the chance of getting any transportation home was slim. So we thought about hiking home but because of the baby, I had to call a friend to pick us up and take us home.

Luckily, he was available. When I thought about hiking with the other two kids, it would have been impossible. They would not be able to walk the remaining journey home—not forgetting that we also had other stuff to carry, such as our pots, grill, water pot, and our bags.

Upon arriving home, everyone took their showers and went to bed. We were too exhausted from the day's activities for a small family talk before bed.

The person in the picture is Curliana Sealys, the third born of my mother Rosalie Sealys and Pierre Polen.

She was born on the 17th of July 1991 and departed this world on the 7th of June 2016.

She was a mother of two, a daughter, granddaughter, niece, cousin, aunt, sister, and a friend.

Her sudden death left a void in many of our hearts.

The news of her death shocked the community. Everyone was in disbelief and many struggled to understand.

Pain and sadness covered our small community and family like a cloud. It was incomprehensible how someone could die from only one episode of a seizure. As the family waited for a post-mortem result, it did not stop others from speculating and spreading their different versions of what happened.

Small communities are always laced with their share of gossip and rumors. If fact-finding and tale whispering should ever stop, the community vibes and busy life would cease. It is almost like a one-stop shop to learn about other people's business, because most persons in the community know each other and therefore assume that whatever is going around in the "gossip circles" must be factual. Whether the story is true or not it will spread like wildfire. But one thing is for sure, this doesn't stop the community support when it calls for it.

I never saw it coming. There wasn't any sign or notice. No warning.

It took me by surprise as it did everyone else. I know death happens but never knew the exact feeling that accompanied it.

I felt guilty and afraid of the feeling that came with it. Many times, I questioned whether I showed my sister enough love. Or if the time I spent with her was enough. Was I good enough at being her sister? What could I have done differently or better? All I had left to remind me of her are the pictures.

The deep void she left can never be filled. I never imagined it would be this way, that she would leave us so suddenly.

My face lights up with a smile as I reflect on the day she made her grand, yet, quiet entrance into our lives. I was only 12 years old when I met her for the first time. The day she came home from the hospital I was excited. I would lay awake watching her with that protective spirit vowing to keep her safe. But I failed, and the promise was broken the day she died. I would never have imagined she would be the first to leave us so heartbroken and sad.

My sister Curliana was the third of my mother's children. Though I was a child at the time, I would help my mother bathe and feed her. I would babysit while my mother did the house chores, and after I had completed the small task she had given me.

We grew up together in a single-parent household with my sister, brother, mom, and myself. We were a tightly knitted family, and the three of us were inseparable. When my sister was a few months old, I took her everywhere. She was like my living doll.

During school days, I would take her to my grandmother before school and then pick her up on my way home from school. This enabled my mother to work overtime to provide for us. Mom would typically leave home at 6:30 a.m. and return at 6 p.m., sometimes 7.

At the tender age of two, my sister stayed with my grandmother full time as I was in secondary school. I was 14 years old at the time. Therefore, the schoolwork was consuming most of my time. It was challenging to get ready for school and take my baby sister to Grandma, so it was more time-efficient for my sister to stay with her.

This allowed me to focus on track and field as I was one of the star athletes at my school. I had signed up with a sports club called Upton stars, and most time after school, I would make my way to the Vieux Fort Comprehensive School's playground for training. I enjoyed running and I would never miss training. During my time in the club, I participated in games such as the Winnera Games, M&C Games, and B&D Games.

My sister was always the quietest and most reserved of my mother's children. She seldom spoke to anyone outside our family circle. Her words were few, but her smile was contagious. She was unique.

Her best friend was grandma with whom she would speak at length. However, if anyone dared to show up during their heart-to-heart conversation, she would withdraw into a silent mood until it was just her and Ma again.

I have fond memories of my sister as an excellent cook and lover of making local jams, which she would sell. This was a skill she learned from our grandmother. My grandmother sells at the market some weekdays and most Saturdays. From the time my sister was five years old, she would accompany her there on Saturdays.

I remember those short trips when I would get my goodie bags already prepared for me by her. I miss the aroma of her food cooking as I approach granny's house.

On my visits, we would spend time in complete silence just sitting in each other's company. Although no words were spoken, we could hear each other's heartbeat while enjoying our time together. Those silent moments were golden as I got to experience the genuine warmth of her heart.

Whenever I picture the road leading to granny's house, I can't help but reminisce the long, lovely walks I had with my sister back to Grandma's place and the enjoyment we had picking fruits around the house. I can almost taste those juicy mangoes, golden apples, yellow plums, sugar apples, just to name a few—what a time we used to have.

My siblings have unique memories of our beloved sister and what she did with them together. That's their story to tell. We thank God for those sweet moments.

I want to forget that dreadful wee hour of the morning when a pain so sharp confused my body and brain and left me struggling to understand the impact it caused on my life. But it will always be part of my journey and first-hand encounter with grief. That morning, the battle began, and it kept hitting me at the speed of light, making me barely able to recover from its hold and position in my life.

Time stood still for the first time in my life. It failed to move forward as my heart pounded in agony, unable to come to terms with the news. At 5:30 p.m. on June 7, 2018, I received a telephone call from my daughter and mother with the most devastating news. My 23-year-old sister had passed away. It was the last thing I expected to hear. I could not believe it. I had spoken to my sister that morning, and she was not sick. In fact, she was fine. That morning, after we spoke, she left the house to do her civic duty and vote during the general elections in our country.

If only I had answered that call earlier, she would have still been alive. If I was available, she may have made it. If she had gotten to the hospital earlier, she would have received the extra care she needed from a professional.

I remember the phone kept vibrating in the pocket of my uniform, which I ignored because I was working at the time and could not answer. After the phone rang persistently, I answered. Looking at the caller ID, I knew instantly, something was wrong. My family doesn't usually call me that late and so persistently. They know I am at work and can't answer my phone most of the time.

I answered. On the other end, my daughter was in tears while relating the message to me.

"Curliana is having a seizure," she said. "We can't get her to reply to us, and there's blood coming from her mouth. We called for an ambulance but were told there isn't any available to come to us because it's the night of the election."

"How long was she having the seizure?" I replied.

"Less than a minute. I think it wasn't long. We just can't get her to wake up."

"Hang up and try calling 911 again," I told her.

When I ended the call with my daughter, I called Raf.

"Hi, are you busy?"

"No," he said, "just watching the election results."

"Do me a favor," I said.

"Sure," he said

"Can you please take my mother to the hospital?" Curliana is not well.

"Yes," he said.

Immediately, I called my daughter back.

"Raf is coming. He will take mummy and Curliana to the hospital," I told her.

Raf didn't live far from my mom. In less than five minutes, he was at my mother's house. I timed them and when I believed they had arrived at the hospital, I called to find out if my sister had regained consciousness. That was when I was told that the doctors were attending to her.

My mind was too occupied to pray, so I simply said, "Lord, help my family." I hung up the call and returned to assist my patient.

In less than an hour, my phone rang. I quickly explained to the patient that I had a family emergency and asked if she would mind if I took a call.

"Go ahead, my sweetheart. I will ring the bell if I require any further assistance," she said.

I left the patient's room to answer my phone without any further delay.

I was hit by utter disbelief at what had just been echoed in my ears. Though I tried to silence the scream from my inner being, it could not be contained. I was shattered, confused, shocked, and lost, engulfed by a sea of unfamiliar emotions. My tears welled up as floodgates threatened to drown me. I tried to breathe, but I couldn't because every breath was cut short by the explosion of unheard screaming.

A lump formed in my throat closing my nasal canal barely leaving any space for air to escape. With every tremble of my lips, I swallowed hard in the hope of not letting it show. I bit my lips against each other in a successful attempt to hold the scream back.

As the strength left my body, my legs jerked, and my frame viciously collapsed under me sending me crashing to the floor below.

My hands quickly replied by punching the carpet in a desperate attempt to ease my pain. The harder I punched the sharper the needle-like pain became, and it stabbed brutally at my heart.

My ears received the sound of my blood rushing from my heart like that of an overflowing riverbank in response to the pain crushing it into bits. For an instant, I wasn't sure I would even survive. I felt powerless as if my heart was attacking itself to save me from myself.

Numbness took over as I tried to mask the pain of mixed emotions posing questions. At that moment, my confusion and shock caused a short encounter with memory loss.

Sweat covered my body. I could not understand how this could happen. Denial, anger, and frustration all visited me at once, and there I was, lost at sea ready to be washed away by a strong wave. That could not be happening. Not to me. Not my sister and not my family.

I froze.

I lost all the will and energy to continue working. I was too confused to concentrate. I was speechless. My mind was speaking but my mouth would not open to let the words escape.

On my knees, I glanced out the window and all I could see was the dark, starless sky. I thought I would only need a moment and then I would be able to carry on.

I saw a shadow coming toward me from the corner of my eyes that broke the stillness in the room. The silhouette stood right in front of me and, as I slowly lifted my head, I realized the vacant, comfortable chair slightly left of the glass double door. A non-gesture was made for me to take a seat on the cream leather chair. I moved toward it and sat down.

The tears kept streaming down my chin, and I could not find the words to tell my co-worker what was wrong. I was offered a cup of tea, but I just had no appetite for tea or water. I kept looking, but I could not register what was happening around me.

A great sense of guilt surrounded my thoughts. I felt I had let my family down. When they needed me, I wasn't available. There I was, saving other people's lives, while my sister was dying. I was useless to them. I could not save my sister. Yet, it is something I know how to do.

My thinking was interrupted when my colleagues suggested we inform the manager. We called her, and she came in early. One of the staff members drove me home. It was so quiet in the car I could hear myself breathing. We did not utter a word to each other and, for once, I was speechless, lost for words. Talking could not help the situation at the time.

On arriving at my flat, I called home to ensure the message I received wasn't a silly prank.

It wasn't.

Three of my friends came over later that day to check on me. They also brought food to ensure I ate. I tried, but I could not swallow. Calmness filled the room as they just sat with me in silence and allowed me to cry without talking. Their presence made me feel safe at the time, but when they left, it was a different story. I was playing mind games with myself.

I was angry at God and very bitter in my heart. So, I sat in the company of my silence and asked God some questions. We had a heart-to-heart talk, but I was the only one talking.

I needed to vent, so I asked Him: "God, how can You do this to us? Why my sister?

Don't You realize she has two small kids who are only 3 years and 6 months old? How could You? Couldn't You let her fulfill her dreams, Lord? She has so many unaccomplished dreams and desires. Is that fair?"

It was hard being alone in my room the next few days before I traveled home to be with my family. I was the only one in my family in the UK at the time and I had to mourn alone. Sleep was distant and my battle with grief was endless.

I managed to travel back to St. Lucia on June 12, 2016. Obviously, it was not a happy, exciting trip like the previous one. This time it was a different kind of trip. I was greeted by friends and family members who worked at the airport. This time, the greeting was not the usual, "Welcome home." I was welcomed with "Accept my condolences. We heard what happen and we are very sorry for your loss."

I was forced to acknowledge that pain again for a short while. Other curious well-wishers greeted me with the question, "How did she die?" Which I quickly dismissed with, "I don't know as yet."

Waiting at the airport to be picked up, I was full of anxiety and growing increasingly impatient. I believe I may have called my pick-up a few times to ensure he was on his way. Thank God, my cousin worked at the airport at the time and waited with me until I was picked up. She deliberately engaged me in conversation to help me relax a bit.

I finally got picked up and the drive seemed very short.

The moment I stepped foot into the family home, all the emotions came back to life. For a moment or two, I felt as if I was in a shipwreck navigating my way through the waves of hidden tears and fear.

Seeing my mother and that look on her face melted my heart into thousands of pieces. I thought to myself, back to square one again, but I could not let it show. I had to be there for my mother. I had to be her strength. I quickly hugged and reassured her that it would all be okay. I embraced her for a moment without exchanging any words. Feeling her arms around me took me right back to my childhood when she would hug me while I was sick; she would pull my body into her chest.

As I moved further into the house, I caught sight of my grandmother in the corner of my eyes. The sadness enveloped her face as she greeted me and said, "You're here, my child." To which I answered, "Yes, ma'am, I made it and the flight was fine."

As the family came together, I could see that everyone was in deep pain from the loss of my 23-year-old sister. My grandmother, who raised Curliana, and to whom she was a companion was deeply hurt.

Everyone was encouraging me to be strong for my mother. So I resorted to masking my emotions. Even though I was present physically, I became invisible. My emotions never mattered; therefore, I was the strong one. My smile overpowered my hurts, aches, and need for comfort.

I believe the people in the community looked at me as the superhero of my family because I was a soldier and a nurse.

The support from the community and family was a great source of comfort as this meant the family seemed happy with a touch of laughter every now and then. Men, young and old had conversations over a friendly game of dominoes and cards with the occasional misunderstanding and cheating.

The kitchen and living room areas came alive with the chattering sound of the ladies' voices deep in conversation while fixing something to eat. Those tastes of fried bakes and salt fish or tuna fish at times were the snacks at night. I looked forward to eating and so did everyone else. The fried bakes were often accompanied by a lovely cup of bush tea. Other nights, it only took a few minutes, and a pot of food was bubbling over on the stove top.

My best friends Nasse and Jacqueline visited every night, and we would engage in conversations. Norlina would call me every day from the USA to talk and cheer me up, and if the others were around at the time, she would reminisce about school days.

Among our visitors were my mother's church family, who would uplift our spirits with songs of praise. Not forgetting the children sometimes asleep or other times sitting comfortably on my mother's lap or some other aunty's lap. At other times, they would be playing with each other in one of the rooms or disturbing the men playing the games.

After our guests left for their various homes, we were forced to remember, and the tears from my mother, grandma, and siblings would flow again.

The sobbing, the wailing, the crying, not a dry eye in sight but one, the eyes of the one forced to look on through a blurry lens in total silence—me.

During that season of my life, I kept busy to avoid the feelings I encountered every now and then. My best method of coping at that time was taking the lead on everything: the arrangement of the service, choosing the casket, building the tomb, etc. Therefore, when emotions surfaced, I quickly pushed them aside. My best friends were my support system. They kept me talking and laughing at silly stuff.

I was mindful of what people might say or think and also to not hear the three common phrases, "She will be okay." "She is in a better place," and "God knows best."

Silently, I wondered how God, who is supposed to know best, allowed these babies to grow up without their mother. Why allow them to enter this world only to leave them without her?

Imagine the pain of losing a sister suddenly but on top of it, having to care for the kids, having a toddler in the house while planning the funeral. They kept me so busy, I had no time to feel the pain. I was just going through the motions.

We had to be there for her babies. They were too young to understand or know what even took place. But we did it and we managed; a superpower became available. When I looked at those two adorable faces, I had no choice but to choose to put pain on the back burner and press forward.

If I ignored the feeling now, it would go away and it would not matter anymore. I adapted quickly to my new role as their mother. My priority was their happiness, joy, and comfort, and I did it all because I owe it to my sister.

Indeed, there's no handbook on grief and, as it turns out, I learned that loss and grief hit us in waves. You learn how to navigate your way through it without hesitation. No two days are the same. The most common misconception of grief is believing after the beautiful funeral service the pain goes away. It is all over, and things go back to normal again. I thought so too. But I was wrong, terribly wrong.

It was just the beginning of things to come. Trying to grieve quickly was the worst thing to consider. It is a path no one should endeavor to take.

We all grieve differently, and every experience is different. I failed to divert from the course because I wanted to be there for everyone but myself.

Back in England with no immediate family around took its toll on me. I was slowly turning into a workaholic. That was my method of coping, and it helped me to avoid my grief and pain. I used the kids as the reason I was working these excess hours, but truthfully, I could not face the reality of my sister's death alone at home. In the back of my mind, I said I was working to help provide for the kids, but the truth is, it was my way of easing the hurt.

When I called home, she was no longer there to parade the kids in front of the laptop during our regular skype calls. I miss her soft smile. I miss seeing her face. I miss Curliana every time I see her children's faces. Every time I see them, it hurts. Her son is a photocopy of her and the more he grows the more he resembles her. Our family is never complete on birthdays, Christmas, Easter, and all the other holidays. St. Lucia's Independence Day always reminds me of that day at the beach.

During those sleepless nights, I had a lot of time to think, but the dialogue in my head was driving me insane. Trying to avoid those thoughts was total madness. When sleep came, it was often in the form of a power nap, something my grandmother often refers to as a cat nap, too short to count.

I hated the fact that Curliana was no longer around to celebrate her son's first birthday. Trying to maintain the custom of the first birthday where parents go all out, we gave him an elaborate party as a way of honoring my sister's memory. This gave me a sense of fulfillment.

She missed his first steps, first teeth, first words, pretty much first everything. Knowing Jerbarry would never see his mother's beautiful smile was heart-breaking.

Losing a sibling is not easy. I always thought we would grow old together and enjoy many memorable occasions.

Before my sister's death, we were planning my mom's surprise 50th birthday party, which was supposed to be in September of that same year. It never happened. There was too much sadness, the brokenness of heart, and heaviness to celebrate three months after my sister passed. As much as we tried to persuade Mom to celebrate her birthday, she would not. She always found an excuse, so we honored her wishes.

Mother's way of dealing with Curliana's death was to make her way to my sister's grave whenever she went to a funeral service at the cemetery. At times, I would find her talking to her. She attended so many funerals, so she could have her moments with my sister at the cemetery.

I have no idea how my other siblings felt. We never sat down as a family and openly discuss what we were going through. We avoided talking about our sister's death other than to say we miss her. That was the most we would say. We all hid our emotions.

I know they were hurting and carried the heaviness in their hearts. The sobbing and wailing spoke volumes. The pain was there but it was shut away in silence. I will never know. I never took the time to ask.

I printed a few pictures of my sister which are part of my home decoration. Every morning and night I enter my living room, I glance at the picture frame just to remind myself of her beautiful smile and the person called my sister.

All I have to remind me of her is a picture in a frame that holds many memories. It reminds me of the love that once lived there. It reminds me of the disagreements we never had, the time we spent together, the laughter, joy, pain, and tears. It also reminds me of the things we could, should, and would have done. But most importantly, it reminds me of my beloved sister and the time we shared.

Curliana Sealys is forever in our hearts.

Chapter Takeaways

1. Put a picture in a frame. The photo represents a beautiful memory that you made with your lost loved one. Make memories with your family. Do not miss family time together. You never know when you may lose them. Be intentional about creating memories with those who are alive.

2. Put the picture frame in a place where you can see it. Every day that you see the photo, it is a reminder of your loved one when he/she was alive and well. Looking at the photos may help you to fill the void of his/her presence. So instead of feeling as if the person is forever gone, you feel as if he/she is still with you.

3. Intentionally focus on the beauty and love relationship that you experienced with that person every time you look at the photo. Those memories will most likely help you shift from pain to love.

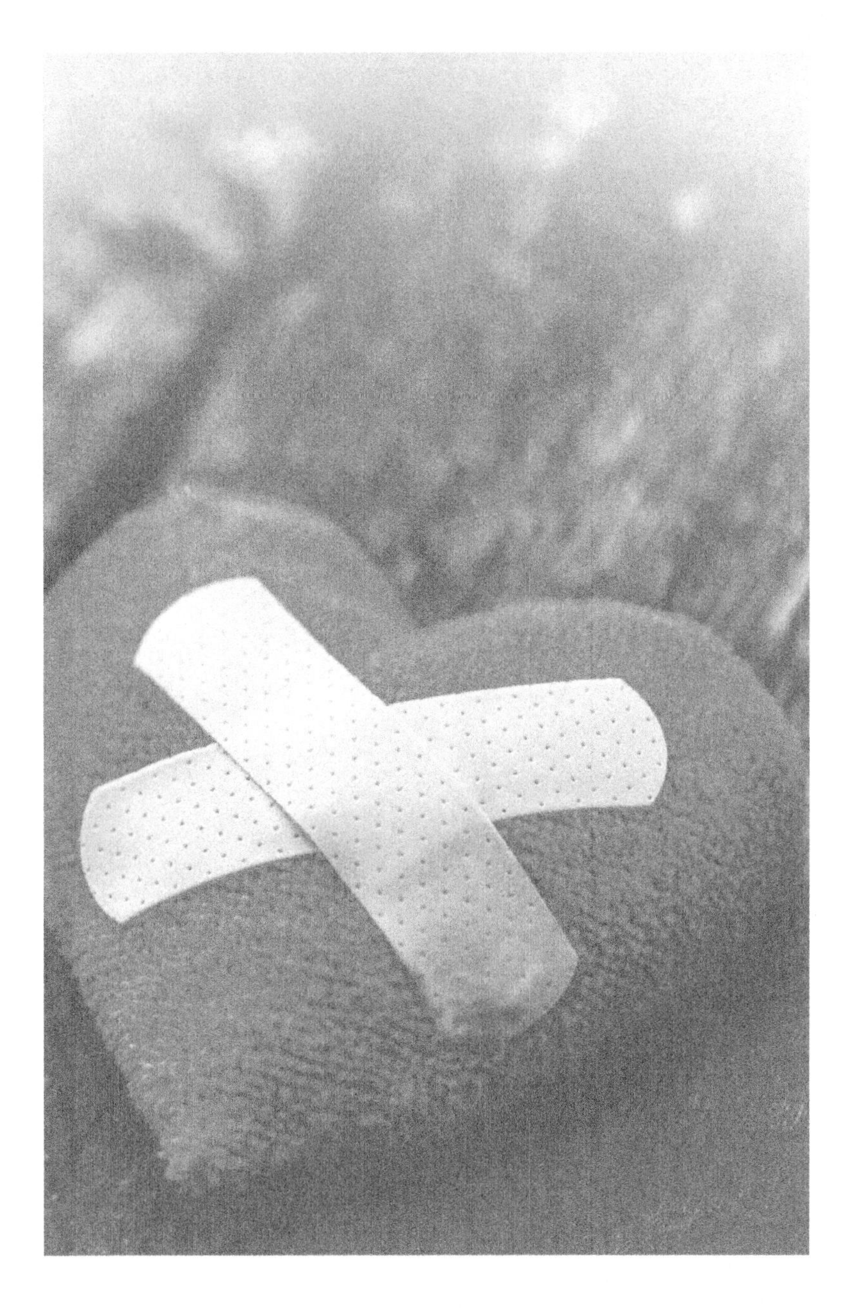

CHAPTER 2

Surrounded by Death

"Everything has a beginning and an end.
Life is just a cycle of starts and stops. There are ends we don't desire, but they're inevitable, we have to face them.
It's what being human is all about."
—**JET BLACK**

Death is inevitable. It happens every day in the world around us and cannot be escaped. If we could avoid death, many people would be alive today. None of us can pay to extend our lives and, quite frankly, from the day of our birth, we are at risk of dying. Research says that every 2 seconds, someone dies around the world.

It is virtually impossible to open our social media without reading RIP. Whether we know the person or not that has become the familiar story on our feeds.

If we are honest with ourselves, we would admit we are all afraid of dying. We all prepare for everything else in life but not its end. Everything has a beginning and an end. So how is it that few of us get ready for the end? We are all guilty of this, including me. The only time we are involved in the grand planning of the end of life is when someone close to us dies.

We are forced to take part in the funeral arrangements, the time when we say our final goodbyes. We plan the service, but we have no idea if it is what the individual wanted—flowers, songs, clothing, eulogy, and casket. We are clueless about the person's preferences because we never discussed them.

Everything on that day, no matter how lush it looks, is 99 percent what we think the person wanted, not what we knew for sure.

We are fully aware death will happen someday, but we are not ready for it to knock at our front doors. Death does not discriminate. It has no mercy on anyone regardless of sex, age, political status, or net worth. Some die sooner than others, but we all die.

I know from experience when death came, I wasn't ready. I wasn't prepared for the effect it would have on my life. I still can't accept that it has happened to me, not once but many times.

I know what it is like to attend funeral after funeral. I have gotten used to the sound of wailing and groaning. I can recall how many eulogies I've had the pleasure of writing and the number of leaflets we had. Not forgetting the many times I have seen a casket or coffin close on the face of someone I know who I would not see again for a while.

Every time it happened the feeling was different. I thought it would hurt less, but the pain increased each time. My family and I were caught in a death trap, and it was determined to cause us unnecessary pain. The web of pain, guilt, and shame just kept weaving us in.

The death of a loved one can happen unexpectedly through an accident or unknown cause. Others may die expectedly from long-term illnesses. Either way, it is hard for those left behind to pick up the pieces of our hearts and move on.

Many have the hope of seeing their loved ones again. I am looking forward to that day when I can hug mine at the second coming of Christ. As a Christian, I believe I will be reunited with my mother and sister but until then, my heart aches every time I think about them.

I know death from both angles: personally and professionally. It sometimes feels as if I am caught in a web, a giant spider web, and the more I try to free myself from it, the more I keep getting trapped again. There's no escape and no way to set me free.

Growing up on the Caribbean island of St. Lucia from birth until I was 12 years old, I lived in an extended family community surrounded by love. I spent most of my childhood with family members while my mom, a single mother, worked odd jobs to provide for me and others in the household. We did not have the most refined things, but we had each other.

The house I grew up in did not have any source of electricity other than a battery-powered generator. Water for cleaning came from the spring and rainwater, while drinking water came from the standpipe on the main road.

Our daily chores involved going to collect water before and after school and washing dishes. Sometimes we would go to the spring to wash and bathe with my grandma. Sometimes we spent Sundays by the river washing and bathing. This was fun as we would meet our friends there.

Sometimes, my mother and aunt would hang the clothes on the bushes and stones to dry. This made it easier for us to carry them back to the house as we normally walked to the river. There was a shortcut at the back of our house, which we used. On our way, we would stop to pick mangoes, golden apples, and other fruits for our journey. At the river, we would pick some more mangoes and coconuts. I enjoyed climbing the trees and standing on a big stone in the middle of the river and then jumping into the water.

We usually walked to school. I hated walking the road on a rainy day as my school shoes would often be covered with mud before we got to the main road. We would stop to clean our shoes under the standpipe and then make our way to the school. Most mornings, we would meet our friends along the way and chat and play to our classes.

Childhood was the most enjoyable time of my life. We played hide 'n seek, cricket, rounders, skipping, and jackstones with my cousins who were my best friends. We were happy. Those moments were priceless. Though we did not have much, we made the best out of what we had. We would play from dawn to dust. That was our only form of entertainment as we had no television. All we had was a battery-operated radio, which my uncles and grandfather used to listen to cricket and the news.

My grandmother's one-bedroom house seemed to get bigger at night to accommodate us during our sleepovers. The living room that wasn't any bigger than our kitchen was our bedroom for the night with five to seven children lying on the floor.

Those days sleeping on the floor were the most comfortable time I have ever slept. Yes, I have slept rough, and I know what it feels like to sleep on just a mat and a camping bag as part of my military training. So, on the contrary, sleeping on granny's hard wooden floor was considered a luxury.

Granny would carefully layer the old clothes to make our bedding for the night. Sometimes before bed, we would gather around the fire, roasting corn, playing games, and telling stories under the moonlight. This kind of storytelling is known as folk-tales in my native culture.

My favorite game was one where you had to guess the number of corn seeds in the other person's hand. It goes like this: "Mother hen laid eggs. How many eggs are in my hand?"

It sounds better in my native language. The aim is to end up with the most roasted corn seeds.

"A ring, a ring o› roses, a pocket-full o' posies" and the chanting of similar songs in games carried on throughout the night under the skies illuminated by the moon and stars. Those were careless moments of my innocent years as we recited "twinkle twinkle little star" and "hey diddle diddle" at the top of our voices interrupting the adults' conversations.

Other nights we would sit with the candlelight reading or helping each other with homework. Though my grand-mother's education never made it further than primary school, her mathematics skills were on point, and she would help us learn the timetables. Her mental calculation always fascinated me. I could never understand how she worked the sum so fast and effortlessly.

We hardly ever went to bed without prayer time at my grandparents' house with my cousins, uncles, and aunties. That was a nightly thing, which no one dared to miss. Psalm 23 and the Lord's Prayer were recited verbatim.

Growing up was never dull. We always had something to do that would keep us occupied or busy. I would not trade this country life for a million dollars.

On school vacation, we would spend most of the morning on the banana farm doing odd jobs for Grandpa in exchange for money to buy some of the things we needed for school when it reopened. I also spent some of the school holidays in Castries where I would attend summer school with aunty Carol at Ave Maria Primary School. I developed my skills in art and craft, storytelling, and poetry there.

Christmas Day was my favorite. All the family would spend the day at my uncle's house celebrating with lots of laughter, singing, storytelling, and dancing. That was when everyone put any differences aside and came together as one to fellowship and socialize. That was an attribute I always admired about my family. Though some of my uncles and aunties were from different mothers, on that day, you would not have noticed.

The love of the family was so warm, and I knew we all belonged. Nothing could break that bond between my mother and her siblings and my cousins and me.

My Cousin's Brutal Death

We felt the ruthless hand of death in 2009. I called home, and my mother said, "You called just in time. I was just going to call and tell you about your cousin's death."

His death was all over the media. So after hearing from my mother, I used a computer at the university's library and went on YouTube to get more information. The clip read "Decomposed Body Found in Vieux Fort North." I was stunned.

I stared at the computer screen with tears streaming down my face. As I watched, I saw his mother with her hands on her head screaming, "My child! My child! Through tears, I could still recognize the faces of many of those who went to see his body. You could see the disbelief on their faces.

It was heart wrenching watching the grief and sorrow as my uncle tried to talk in an interview. All he could say was "Yes, that's my son" repeatedly. My eyes were fixed on the shirtless man in his black pants shaking his head as he tried to find words to explain what he was feeling but was muted by the wails of his partner. He could not say anything but those four words, "Yes, that's my son." After watching the YouTube news clip, I went to my lecturer and explained I had to leave early because of a family emergency.

The train journey home seemed longer than usual and very quiet. The always busy, talkative commuter was missing for once, or so I believed. I was preoccupied with my thoughts. I shut out the noise of others around me, and there I was, in a new world that I created in my mind to take away the feelings I was going through. I was miles away from my family with no one to hug and comfort me.

I craved a hug and someone to say it's okay. Keeping all this to myself was too much to bear. As I turned the key to my flat and entered the room, the stillness of the walls spoke to me. For a moment, I thought I was crazy. Dropping my laptop and books, I went into my bedroom and cried on my silk-covered pillow alone. I was no longer hungry; I just wanted to sleep.

My mother is my cousin's godmother and aunty. He would always come over to our house on his way to school or from the shop. He would never pass our home without stopping. Mom would make sure he had already eaten, and if it was too late to go home, he would spend the night and then go home the following morning.

My cousin was only twelve years old when his decomposed body was found by one of the farmers. My uncle did not know his son was missing. He thought he was at his elder sister's home. He did not know she had sent him home three days earlier. His life was taken away from him prematurely.

The track to his house was a beaten path through the plantation full of bananas and other crops. You had to cross a spring of fresh, flowing water to get home. I always stopped to look at the sea on the horizon. The scene was breath-taking. Who would think such horror would exist under its beauty?

The path was usually safe and lined mainly by houses. But sometimes, the bananas, coconuts, and other trees made it hard to see past the hedges. The community, which was mostly made up of family members was in shock when my cousin's body was found in the wild.

How could someone do something so heartless to a 12-year-old? We saw this type of thing in the movies or on international news, not in this small community where everyone knew each other. The hand of death brought with it a turmoil of pain and sadness, a dark cloud that lingered for days. The last entry of my cousin in my photo album was a picture of him, my sister, daughter, and me at their First Communion at the Pierrot church.

The news that he was murdered did not ease the pain but invited more questions than answers. Sad to say, as I write, the answer was never found, and no one was held responsible for his death. As expected, the community was rampant with rumours and gossip about what might have transpired.

Someone killed my cousin, but we have no idea who the killer is. It's a mystery, no one has been arrested, and we have not found closure.

The murder changed our community. The children who once walk to and fro without thought were too afraid to go anywhere or walk the road alone. The road they often walked when going to my grandmother was no longer a route they wished to travel. My daughter could not sleep; she was afraid of seeing my cousin.

I was angry and kept replaying all the possible scenarios in my head. I wanted them to find the person and make him pay for my cousin's death. Why did this evil coward prey on a kid? What was the motive behind the murder of a child? How could someone be so heartless? What did my cousin do to deserve that?

My uncle became a heavy drinker. Ever since that day, he was constantly intoxicated with alcohol and would stay out all night blaming himself for the death of his son. He wanted revenge but did know who to take it out on.

When I saw those dark lines around his eyes, I knew he was hurting, but I could not take his pain away. I could only pity him. His speech did not make sense anymore and it was just a waste of time trying to converse with him. He never received any counseling or help from the police or any organization. We had no idea where to turn for help and how to deal with this situation.

Thankfully, when I went home for my mom's funeral, my uncle told me he had given up drinking and was sober.

Fast forward to February 2, 2022, almost thirteen years later, my uncle was once again mourning the loss of another son.

Dave died in a vehicular accident. Prior to this accident, he was crippled after being hit by a fire truck. He learned to move around on his hands and bottom. His disability did not hinder him from getting from point A to point B. He could move faster than I on two feet.

It was a sad day when I heard of his passing. We will always remember you, my cousin.

Walking along the shore of the golden gritty sand enveloping my feet, I stopped to admire the orange light of the sunset where it met the lining of the sea. I was taken back to my childhood many years ago, which I dare not forget.

The sound of adults chatting and looking at their children laughing while playing in the sand—some building sandcastles, others burying each other in the sand. The loudspeakers blasted sweet, melodious music as the crowd sang the familiar words like a choir in the background.

As my eyes stretched further down the beach, several tourists lazed around absorbing the sun. Some were horseback riding, while others enjoyed bathing in the warm waters or zipping around on jet skis in the open ocean. This was a usual Sunday spot and well-known for beach parties back in the day.

The delicious smell of chicken and fish roasting on the grill filled the air as families sat enjoying the meals. My cousin and I were too busy enjoying the water and trying to ride the waves to eat, so we would wait until we were hungry or one of the adults called us out.

Our picnic bag contained a tray of macaroni and cheese, fig salad, rice, and some ground provisions such as yam and dasheen, delicious and mouth-watering meals made by my mother and her sisters. Many times, we would share with other friends and family members who came to join us later at the beach. We quenched our thirst with ice-cold homemade lemonade and water.

We would stay on the beach with my mother and aunties, while my uncles went fishing in the mangrove. Indeed, they never returned empty-handed. They would have bags of freshwater fish, which I recall took hours to clean when we got home.

Often, we would end the evening with lovely, golden fried fish and bakes covered in ketchup. For me, that was the secret ingredient at the time. Not to forget the long walk back from the beach hitch hiking a ride to the nearest point. Sometimes, if we were lucky, we got one that took us home.

Another Life Taken Too Soon

That beach holds a lot of childhood memories. It is also where the burned car with my cousin's ashes in the trunk was found. This was another incident that I saw on HTS News online. When I recognized my uncle, I immediately grabbed my keys and coat and left my flat.

It took me less than ten minutes to get to the corner shop where I purchased an international calling card to call home.

WhatsApp and Facebook did not exist at that time and the only means of communication was via calling cards or a pay phone. The Internet was not yet available in the area and very few people had mobile phones.

My call was to confirm what I had already known. Yet another life was taken too soon. Her life was cut short by another. I still hold that image I saw on my computer screen in my head. I could see the family and her boyfriend's family standing beyond the blue and white tape marked "Police." As I scanned the crowd, I saw my mother, aunt, and uncles.

Their faces spoke a thousand words of pain and sadness they were forced to acknowledge. There was no body to look at. They could not touch her and say, "Yes, that's my daughter; that's my cousin; that's my son." All they had were the silver-grey ashes of my cousin and her boyfriend.

The sad thing is that she did not have a proper funeral because it was just ashes. There was no body to view, no one to say goodbye to. Was she raped before they burned her? We will never know. Did they kill her and her boyfriend first or burned them alive?

I believed I prayed the most for my uncle and family at that time. My cousin did not deserve to die like this. She was young and still had her whole life ahead of her.

I believe God gave us strength as a family. Yet again, we never talked about the grief we were dealing with, so with time, it seemed to be forgotten. We now had this moment where grief was replaced with happy moments such as the birth of a baby, graduation, weddings, etc. These were moments of great joy and celebration of life, rather than the cold hands of death.

Death Everywhere

Death just kept coming. Every couple of months, every year, it tugged at our hearts and pulled them apart.

Eight months after my sister died in 2016, I lost my aunty in 2017. Every time we thought we were recovering from the loss, someone else died. Consequently, those unhealed wounds opened again and started to bleed.

It felt as if a gust of heavy wind picked me up and pushed me back to the starting line. Sometimes it felt as if there was no end to this storm of life. I've been stuck in a shower with more dark clouds than rain because teardrops never came, but when they did, they never ended.

A month after her death, my aunt's father died, and the family was back in mourning again. For a moment, it seemed as if the only time we came together as a family was at a funeral service.

We were crippled by death; it was everywhere. We buried someone every couple of months in our family circle: cousins, grand aunty, aunties, and an uncle to my grandmother on my father's side. Some died suddenly and others from illnesses and incorrect diagnoses.

My cousin's death in March of 2018 haunted me and caused me to blame myself for a long time. Guilt was eating me up inside because I felt responsible for her death. I had traveled home that year when she called me asking for financial help with the cost of her dialysis. After the birth of her son, she was diagnosed with what the doctors thought was kidney failure and had to start dialysis.

The day my cousin came for the money, I remember telling my mother I didn't believe her kidney was the problem. I questioned my cousin a bit, and she told me the doctors confirmed it was her kidney that had failed. She had already started treatment, so I told her I would meet her at the hospital as there were a few questions I needed to get answered. However, something came up on the day of the treatment, and I could not meet with her as promised.

Before my flight back to England, I gave her some money to cover some of the cost of the treatment and promised to send her more every month. She wasn't just a cousin; she was like my baby sister.

Natalie used to live with my family from childhood and when we built our home, she moved with us also. I covered all her school expenses, including bus fare, shoes, uniforms, and a school bag every year.

I can clearly remember the days and the many hairdos I used to give to her and her sisters for school and our many trips to the farm to carry wood for charcoal making. I can also recall us sitting together enjoying my mother's breakfast, lunch, and dinner. We would walk home from church, the beach, and after visiting family members.

She was part of our family, and my mother never made her feel less than a daughter. She was treated equally to us. If you did not know, you would have thought my mother had given birth to her.

At night, we would all find our comfortable positions on the floor of the living room on mattresses, two joined together to accommodate us. Even though I had come home from

England on holiday, I would still sleep next to them on the living room floor.

We had a special family bond, and, without hesitation, it was just easy to support her financially when I learned she was sick and needed help.

Not too long after I returned, my mother called from the hospital saying that the dialysis port had become infected, and the doctor had admitted my cousin. The family was invited to donate blood as she would need a transfusion.

During that hospital stay, which was her final one, after a more detailed examination, she was diagnosed with lupus. There was a plan to fly her out to Martinique our neighboring island for medical assistance. However, it was too late; she died a few days after. Lupus presents the same symptoms as kidney failure and being treated for it caused more harm than good. I carried that guilt for a long time thinking that I had noticed something, which could have been detected earlier.

I questioned myself a lot, believing if I did not give her the money, she would not have had dialysis and died. Blame me for contributing to her getting the wrong treatment. Had I gone to the hospital that day, it would have made a difference. I had a few questions to ask the doctors. The signs I saw told me it was not kidney failure.

I am sure she would have had more time with her son. I was consumed with more guilt than pain and could not find comfort, only pity for myself. I hated myself for failing her. I did not use my knowledge to save her life. The pain is perpetual. I missed the chance to advocate for her the same way I do for my patients in my care.

Once again, we were mourning the loss of another young soul and yet another motherless baby boy was in our family.

The pattern continued. In the summer of 2019, I lost three family members within weeks of each other: my great-grand-aunt, my cousin, and my grandmother.

I had already planned to visit St. Lucia at the time so I managed to attend the funeral services, except the one held for my grandmother on my father's side. She got buried the day before I arrived.

My great-grandaunt and cousin were buried a few days apart, which allowed us to attend both funeral services. Granny was already 94 years old and bedbound to old age. Although her death was expected, when it happened, it still came as a shock when my dad called to inform me of the news. My granny was a loving woman, and, in the absence of my father, she would ensure that my mother brought me to see her. She did not have much as I can recall but would not let me go hungry. I was always well-fed when I visited. She sold fried chicken, grilled chicken, fish, and fried bakes, and I was the first customer.

The year before when I visited her with my uncle, she was so proud to pull out her photo album and show me my picture. She had one with me in my army uniform and then she asked: "My child, you wonder where Granny took that picture. Your mother gave it to me. I am so proud of you and all you are doing. Keep it up and always remember, no matter what, I love you." She will always hold a portion of my heart.

Not every funeral service is a sad one. My family always takes the opportunity to make each other laugh. With tears in their eyes, they greet each other with a hug and plenty of chatting. The family was the best support network during those painful moments.

My relatives would joke it took the burial of so and so for me to visit. My only remaining great grand uncle would come down south with a bus or two of other relatives we never knew. Though the day was not joyous, we got to meet our cousins and family who we did not know growing up. That was special to us. We had unity amid our storms.

In October 2019, I received another shock when my mother called me to tell me my cousin Sherril had passed away.

"Mom, just a month ago I was with her. What do you mean she died this morning?"

I remember clearly at my great grand aunt's funeral she said, "Give me my hug eh, because you don't know if when you come back, I will be here. I love my family even though we don't meet often. I love you all," she told me that day. "If I haven't told you, my love, you have made the family proud. You are a soldier and a nurse, and I am so proud of you as my own daughter."

She told me our family is very knitted and everyone knows about my achievements and was cheering me on. She reminisced about how she and my mother would talk whenever they met and the trouble they both gave together when they were young.

My relatives were never shy to tell me how proud I made them for breaking barriers they never had the chance to. We would talk for hours encouraging each other. I believe the younger generation missed that bond those before us had.

Our family would talk about their childhood experiences with such passion that you would envy them. They told stories about walking the dark streets with no lights, their days on the plantation, and washing at the river. They talked about our great-great-grandparents with such fond memories that at times, I wish I had met them. We love each other and the love we share money cannot replace. Though poor, they considered themselves rich in love.

My cousin was a happy person and for such, she will always be remembered as the life of the party. She joked about everything and took nothing too seriously. She loved her children. I know she gave them the best she could afford. We all miss her, especially her children.

Christmas Day 2019, was a day when families come together to celebrate, a day that is supposed to be full of joy and laughter. But the sound of Christmas carols was replaced by screaming, shouting, and wailing.

The message I received the morning was "Morning, Babe, Daddy passed."

In shock, I replied: "Oh my, accept my sympathy."

Rafati's dad, my father-in-law, had passed.

As the days went by, I kept messaging and calling to ensure he was okay. When I lost my sister, he and his sisters were constantly there for me. Their support helped me through that ordeal. I was able to express how I felt because Rafati was open and understanding. Now, the table had turned, it was my time to ensure he could express his deepest feelings.

By the time I called my mother to inform her that Rafati's dad had died, she had already left home. She was already with the family as we don't live too far from him. During his short illness, Mummy would spend most evenings at his bedside until Raf or his sisters got home.

He was a pillar in the community and owned the very first shop in the area. Growing up, this was the convenience shop my grandparents would send us to buy the basic items: meat, flour, sugar, soap, etc. The shop still serves the community.

I had to travel home for the funeral service. I owed it to Rafati and his sisters as they have always been by my side and my family's side during our moments of sadness and bereavement. After all, I am part of the family.

Rafati is a great source of support. He shows up for me and always puts my needs and that of my family first. Nothing is too much for him to do for my family. Twice, he was the one available in the absence of emergency transport to take my mother and sister to the hospital. I struggle at times to accept the outpouring of love and support because I am so used to being self-sufficient. He has accepted my family as his own and even in my absence, he is there for them. I feel safe knowing someone is looking out for them, and, for that, I will forever be grateful.

Our family has always been there for each other. Even when their mother died over 20 years ago the connection between the two families was strong. We did many things together. Cathy, Rafati's sister and I would wake up at the crack of dawn with peach dark skies. With time, our eyes got used to the darkness as we carried water from the standpipe to fill the barrels at home with water.

We would go in search of brush to make a broom to sweep the yard and get some mangoes and other fruits along the way. We celebrated many events together: weddings, birthdays, and going to the beach and farm. The support network between his family and mine has always been there and, as the years go by, it has gotten stronger, even with the younger generation.

I am glad I traveled home for that one week in January. Little did I know it would be the last time I would spend with my dear mother, who died a month later. Though it was short, the memories of those days together and the conversations we had are irreplaceable.

The funny thing is when my mother's last child was 20 years old, I went home and found Mom with a three-week-old baby girl. We joked about it saying at that age, when all her children were adults, our mother had a baby.

How did this happen? My mother went to the hospital to visit my uncle and returned with a new-born baby, a bottle, the clothes the baby was wearing, three vests, and ten diapers.

Knowing I was coming home for Mr. Eugene's funeral, she asked me to bring some baby clothes. I did. When I arrived, I met the most beautiful baby girl who we called Miracle. You could not help but fall in love with her—our mother's miracle baby.

My mother had agreed to foster a child. But she never got to see her grow up. She is now two years old.

My mom died suddenly on March 21, 2020. Heartbreak, numbness, and pain—I could have died that day. You will read more about her later.

My Godmother Was Like a Second Mother

A few months later, on November 21, 2020, I lost my godmother. While I was home after my mother's burial, she would just show up at the house to spend time with us.

I would go to her home and then walk back up the road. She would cook food and send it to me. She cooked the best fried fish and dali. She was known for it, and it was what she did to earn a living with her mother. My godmother was like my second mother. I loved her.

During my school years, she would assist my mummy with the purchase of my books. I got toys, clothes, and gifts during Christmas and Easter from her. She took care of me as she did her own children. Growing up, I would often sleep at her house. She loved to crochet, which is something I never learned as a hobby. I found it too difficult to understand.

The last time I talked to my godmother was October 29, 2020, when we walked the street to my grandmother's house. I said goodbye to her on November 2, the day I returned to the UK. I did not know it was my final goodbye to her. May your soul rest in peace Agnes Celise. We miss and love you. It still hurts.

On May 30, 2021, my uncle, also my godfather, passed away. My uncle was often admitted to the hospital. We had no idea this would be his last.

My uncle was like a father to me as I did not grow up with my dad in the home. He played a major role in my life. After my birth, my dad moved to Barbados and started his life over there. There was a lack of communication between my dad and mother as, during that era, phones and the internet weren't available.

During my childhood, I can only recall my father visiting twice, once when I was 15 years old and the other, I am not quite sure how old I was at the time.

My uncle filled the void of me not having a father around. He would show his disappointment if I did something he was not pleased with and provided support when needed. I felt protected around my uncle. I could not comprehend or fault his love. I credit my uncle and other family members for much of my upbringing.

Every time I traveled back home, I made it a priority to spend time with my godfather.

I dedicate this small section to the many other family members who have left us with broken hearts that are slowly healing.

I know the time we spend apart can never replace your love for us.

The tears we cry are just for a while.

The pain we feel is quickly replaced by love.

So we promise to remember the good times and smile every time it hurts.

Though our hearts break, they carry more love than sadness.

Chapter Takeaways

1. It is important to have a support network when you are grieving. Join a support group or speak to persons you trust who you know will not judge you for grieving.
2. Instead of being surrounded by death, you can surround yourself with the love of family members who are alive. Focus on the love and support that you received from those who have passed on and continue the legacy of love and support.
3. Choose to see the positive and be intentional about making shifts that will help you to focus on life instead of loss.

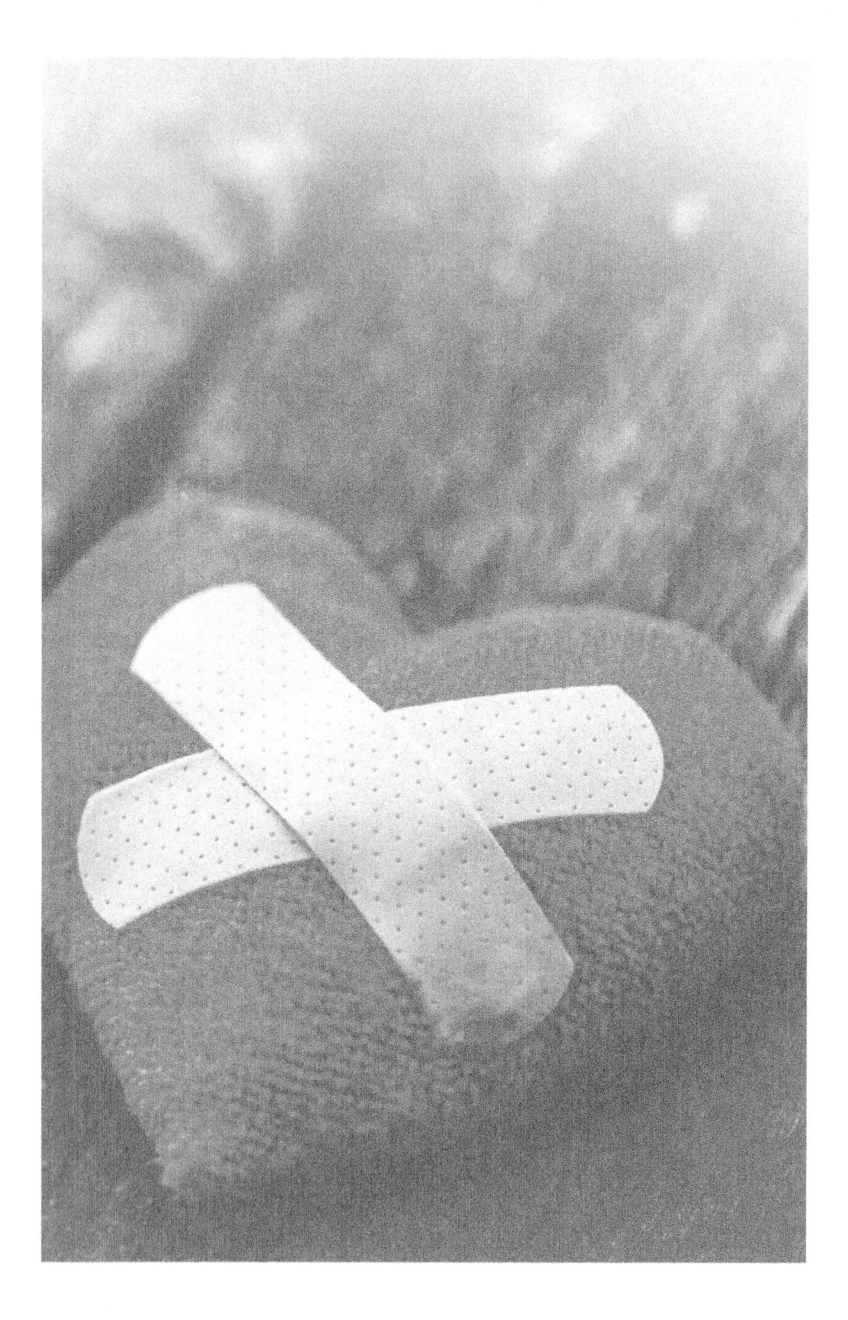

CHAPTER 3

My Grieving Heart

"Blessed are those
who mourn for they shall be comforted"
(MATTHEW 5:4 NKJ)

Grief is an inevitable part of our human experience, and it affects our entire beings emotionally, physically, and psychologically. The time comes when each of us is in this deep sorrow because of death, broken relationships, and other situations in our lives. No one is exempt. However, grief is still taboo in some circles and none of us really talk about it. We do not open up about our feelings for fear of being judged, criticized, or isolated.

Within our society, culture, families, and friendships, we like to fix things and make them better. We like to hide our true feelings and hope time will erase all the pain. But I have learned the hard way that grief cannot be fixed. It is invisible.

I know what grief is like. We have this on and off relationship with no strings attached. So if you are grieving, I understand the feelings of madness you are going through. It can play with your emotions beyond your control and even though you want a way out, it just won't leave.

As you have read, I had a personal relationship with grief and loss for over six years now. The more I tried disconnecting myself from this intense emotion, the more I realized I wasn't strong enough to walk away. The more I tried walking out and disassociating myself from its firm grip, the greater its hold on me. I felt trapped in its net. I was overcome with emotions that would not set me free. I was hiding within the fear of an invisible glass wall, which I had created, and it had consumed me.

Grief introduced itself to me uninvitedly and refused to leave. This stranger moved in with all its baggage and my home was becoming too small to accommodate the two of us. It never told me it came with pain and full of uncertainty. My life was a monopoly of pain.

As the days went by, I felt as if I was cheating on guilt with fear. I was cheating on fear with shame. I was cheating on shame with guilt and guilt with whatever emotions chose to accompany me on the day. I constantly felt guilty. Guilt became my close friend in my darkest hours. Sometimes I disliked the feeling, but I had grown so used to it that when it didn't show, I felt disappointed.

Most of the time, I was in a fog and the battle in my head was the worst. Every single emotion put on the most spectacular display and at times, they won me over with a single flow of tears. Others presented as waves of anger and, as a result, sometimes, I ended up snapping at the wrong person.

Living in the shadows of grief can have this effect on you. It will follow you everywhere you go and consume you with anger, hurt, and confusion. That's how I felt. It would not permit me to think straight, so I failed to realize that my family needed me. They too were in agony.

In a state of deep sorrow, it is easy to retreat to our inner selves. We can only think about our pain, our heartbreak, our loss. At the same time, those we love are also hurting; they have also been heartbroken. As said before, everyone deals with grief differently. And no matter how often we have lost a loved one to death, we can never adequately prepare for it.

It's important that as you grieve, you do not become isolated. If you do, grief will devour you. While you go through the grieving process, though it may be hard, it will help if you reach out to others who are hurt. Pay particular attention to your children as they look to you as an example of how to make it through this painful season of life.

Death teaches us many life lessons. One of them is to never take those we love for granted when they are alive. It's interesting how the simplest things we don't properly appreciate about our loved ones when they are alive are so important to us when they are gone—the person's voice, touch, laughter, the way he/she walked, smiled, and gestured. We long for those moments.

I felt the anguish of not having the one person who would have encouraged and helped me make sense of life around. We could no longer speak as we used to. I needed her and her advice so much. If only I could get one last pet talk. That's all I craved for—only one more.

Beware of Depression as You Grieve

Though grief is a natural response to death and loss, the multiplicity of emotions we go through can cause us to withdraw from the routine and activities we once did. Depression usually steps in when the reality of the person's death hits home. While grieving and staying away from certain things for a while may be a way for some to heal, prolonged depression and isolation are not normal. If you are consistently having trouble sleeping, feeling fatigued, lacking energy, having a poor appetite, and crying endlessly, these are signs that it's time to seek help.

Many mornings I woke up and just did not feel like getting out of my bed. It was a struggle that took every ounce of energy out of me. Sometimes I thought if I stayed in bed, it would make it easier for me to face another day without my mom and sister. Maybe just lying there, disinterested in life, would fill the void. Perhaps when I got up later, I would realize it was just a nightmare and my mom and sister were still with me.

Those mornings I kept my curtain drawn and allowed the darkness to saturate my room. I purposefully used a thicker sheet or towel to keep the light from penetrating inside. Every crack of light that emerged, I would try my very best to conceal it.

The path of grief just kept getting darker and darker. Sleeping was becoming impossible. When I slept, I would wake up crying so I could cry myself back to sleep again. At times, I was afraid to close my eyes because I did not want to dream about my loved ones or see their faces. Alone, I would sit up and gaze blankly at the wall hoping the pain would go.

During my grief, I could not eat for days. Everything was a

challenge. I had no handbook on how to grieve. And the stark reality is grief doesn't end on the day you bury your loved ones. Grief is like that unwanted weed in a beautiful flower garden. The more you pull it out, the more it reappears. It is that stubborn vine that intertwines itself around the flower and will not let go.

It shows up when you are trying to sleep at night, at the breakfast table, in church when your loved one's favorite song is sung and scripture read. Grief shows up on their birthdays, anniversaries, Christmas Day, and all the other special occasions.

Grief shows up when the phone rings and it is not your husband, wife, mother, son, or daughter. It appears when you cook the person's favorite meal. Grief shows up uninvited and unexpectedly and it hurts. Grief can't be killed as you would something physical you are afraid of. It's a tricky emotion; you are never fully prepared for how it makes you feel or how you will handle it.

My brain refused to communicate with the rest of my body. I forgot simple stuff and was blank at times. I felt empty. Although I was having conversations with others, there wasn't much activity going on in my mind. Sometimes, I did not recall anything that happened.

Depression was creeping in, and I hated the feeling. The random biting of my nails and shaking of my legs whenever I was sitting alone, were signs of anxiety. I would try reading as a distraction but the words on the page made no sense to me; they were jumbled. I just could not concentrate on or comprehend it. I feared I was losing the ability to read and that added to my stress.

The anxiety of how to adjust without them bombarded me with questions. I was always wondering if I was doing things right. What would they have done if they were around? Switching places with my mother was never part of the plan so early in my life. At 39 years old, I had to be the mother to my siblings, as well as aunty and grandma to my nieces and nephew.

At first, when my niece said to me. "Aunty, now you are granny, aunty, and mummy," I laughed but I did not realize what was going on in her head. After the death of my mother, sister, and other relatives, I took on more and more responsibilities I did not bargain for.

Overwhelmed by the Burden of Guilt

The guilt was overbearing. Deep within, I felt I had failed my family and blamed myself for many reasons. One of the things that really ate me inside was the fact that I was miles away on another continent. I had a degree in health but my mom and sister both died. I wasn't there to perform CPR or basic first aid that might have saved their lives.

If you have lost a loved one and you are overwhelmed with guilt, you are not alone. Millions of people are struggling with this emotion every day. We feel guilty about all sorts of things, even the irrational. Guilt is real and can cause us to push others away and break up relationships.

Guilt is like a formidable wall that is difficult to break down. We can feel guilty about moving on and forgetting about the ones we love. In fact, this guilty feeling combined with fear can paralyze us.

Though guilt is a common emotion when dealing with grief, you should do everything you can to ease out of its grips, lest it destroys you. Here are a few suggestions to help you get rid of the guilt that has piled up in your life:

- Forgive yourself quickly. Whether the guilt is rational or irrational, forgive yourself. If you did something wrong or your wrongdoing is just a perception, forgive yourself. If you made mistakes, forgive yourself. The point is forgiveness is the best answer to guilt and accusations.

- Go easy on yourself. Guilt always makes you wonder what else you could have done. It keeps you in a state of perpetual doubt, questioning if you did the best you could. It magnifies every act, every word, and condemns you. But most likely, you did the best you could in the circumstances. And if you didn't, acknowledge it. We all err at some time. Focus more on the good things you did, not what you didn't do.

- Accept the person you love is no longer here. And there is nothing you can do about it. I know the thought of this alone is difficult, but if you can bring yourself to this stage, it will help you.

- Learn from your regrets and mistakes. Let them create changes in your priorities, your other relationships, and use them to educate others.

- Think about your loved one. If you could speak to your loved one, what would he/she tell you about the feelings of guilt you carry? Would he/she want you to live the rest of your life crippled by guilt?

Suppressing Grief Is Unhealthy

For six years, I suppressed my grief. Wrestling with the pain it inflicted was like being under the surgeon's knife without anesthesia, feeling every movement of the blade cutting into my heart layer upon layer. That pain is a part of me I wish people could see and feel.

When my sister and mother died, I was angry at them because they never said goodbye. However, I believed I could manage and that was my biggest mistake. I was sinking faster than the titanic. I felt I was in neck-high water in the ocean. Searching for a way out of that ocean, I had to quickly raise my head above the water because of my responsibilities.

I had to be strong and hold back the tears because so many people depended on me to be strong. My heart was bleeding; yet, no one could see. I could not let them. I was not supposed to be weak. I was an ex-soldier and a nurse. Be brave. Dry your eyes and move on.

Instead of dealing with my grief, I busied myself trying to find ways to distract myself, hoping to forget what we were dealing with. I was looking for a way to move on as quickly as possible but that was impossible.

Those around me did not notice I was too far gone with grief and that there was no turning back. I had mastered the skill of grieving in silence. I would show up for work and function as normal. I was physically present but mentally absent. I would laugh and smile, but the emptiness was present.

I never spoke to anyone about these feelings. I kept everything I felt inside. Truthfully, I did not know how to talk about it or bring the topic up. I did not want to be judged or criticized.

I just kept quiet and moved on. Unbeknownst to me, I was causing lots of damage to myself without even realizing it.

Perhaps you are suppressing your grief because you think it's necessary. You have so many responsibilities and if you don't stand strong, you think everything will come crashing down. Or you refuse to express your true feelings because you simply don't know what to do with them, so you put them aside and let them harbor. I can tell you from experience, this is not a good idea. Yes, sometimes, you may need to keep your feelings inside. However, when you do this as a long-term solution, it will wreak havoc in your life emotionally, mentally, socially, and physically. It is unhealthy. I learned this the hard way. Suppressing your grief can have lasting negative effects on your life. Irritability, anger, violent outburst, depression, and anxiety are some of the problems that may develop because you have not allowed the grieving process to take its course.

My relationship with grief did not suddenly come to an end. Some days, when I sat alone, I wept, and other days, I laughed as I reflected on the precious memories of those I love.

As time progressed, I learned to sit with my shadows, as well as the light. That's what accepting grief and loss is like.

I had to let myself feel those emotions, instead of running away from them. Like a rocking boat, I had to take each wave in stride. Finding the light at the end of the tunnel is possible. However, there will be times when shades of darkness will reappear until you are comfortable moving on with fond memories.

Grief will never leave you instantly, so don't expect it to. It's a process, and we all go through it at different stages. Some days, when I lack the willpower to end this relationship with grief, I go with the flow. When sadness comes, I embrace it and when happiness comes, I smile with it. I can now write with a smile on my face, rather than with pain and regret.

"The pain of grief is just as much part of life as the joy of love: it is perhaps the price we pay for love, the cost of commitment."

—DR. COLIN MURRAY PARKES

Chapter Takeaways

1. It is okay not to be okay. It is okay to grieve. Take moments to savor your tears. It does not make you weak; it makes you human.

2. Do not shut the people around you out. It is okay to let them know that you are struggling. Be willing to speak about your emotions. Do not hide behind the words "I am doing fine." Let others know your true feelings.

3. Accept that you need help and be open to receiving support from others. Ensure that you have a network of persons you can reach out to for support and prayer.

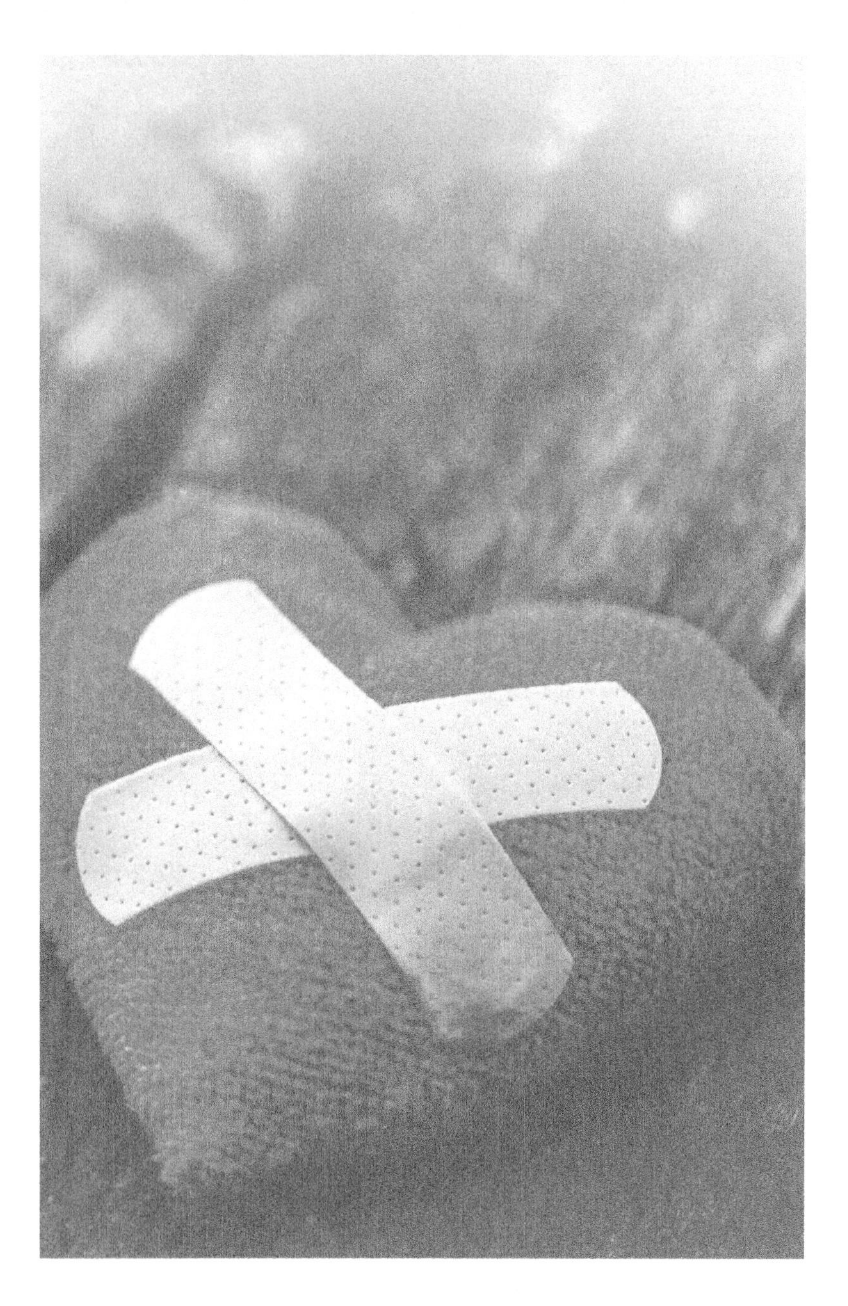

CHAPTER 4

Hidden Tears

"We need never to be afraid of our tears."
—CHARLES DICKENS

Imagine having a job where you call people to share good news with them. Good news—you won a million dollars. You landed your dream job, or you had a new member added to your family. Exciting news! Now, imagine a job that was the opposite. You deliver bad news. Somebody must do it, right?

yourself at the other end of that call. Maybe you can because you have probably been there already. But, if you haven't, be thankful. Imagine picking up your phone and receiving the news your loved one has taken her final breath.

Even though I have been the bearer of bad news to families many times because of my job, being the recipient of that call and getting that kind of news unexpectedly was heart-breaking. Death was becoming all too familiar, in both the professional setting and my personal life. The calls with me on the other end of the line were becoming too frequent.

On March 21, 2020, during the midst of the world's greatest nightmare (the pandemic) in our time, I faced a nightmare of my own. That day is one that I will not forget even if I try. It was the same weekend our boundaries were closed to all incoming and outgoing flights in the UK.

It was also the same weekend people were told to isolate, work from home, and maintain social distance. It was the weekend we started living in a virtual world, but permit me to say, that wasn't the case for us as nurses and other essential workers.

In the middle of that crisis as a nurse, my mother called me daily to ensure we prayed together—every morning and every evening despite the five-hour time difference. She kept me going.

As the death toll increased so did my anxiety and that of my colleagues who were left to work face to face. Several colleagues were considered high risk and, therefore, were asked to stay at home in isolation. Those working in the clinics were to work from home. The world was in total panic. Every country was facing the same nightmare simultaneously. Countries were looking to each other for answers. The coronavirus that was said to have originated in China was spreading globally at a rapid speed, quicker than the speed of light it seemed.

Patients were no longer patients. They were just statistics in the daily news. All over the world, thousands were dying alone in isolation. The busy flow of visitors in and out of the hospital was no more, except for those who came via ambulances with the hope of leaving alive. Many never did.

Their loved ones could not visit and breaking the news to families that their loved ones had died was dreadful. Through cracking vocals of a well-rehearsed line "I am sorry to inform you that your loved one has passed away," we did the best we could.

People were dying faster than we could get the message to their loved ones. A day on the shift hardly went by without the death of several patients. Let me interrupt your thought for a moment. You might be saying, "Surely, this is normal in a hospital." Wrong. These were not normal times. Nothing about this was normal. We were used to saving lives, except for those out of our control. Now, with the COVID-19 pandemic, patients were dying before we could attend to them.

We had no idea how to treat this virus and what it was we were dealing with. This was far from our normal admission. CPR was no longer an option due to the nature of the virus. We had to protect our own lives. We had to survive for our families who were waiting for us to come home.

It seemed we were waiting to fill the bed just to have the patient spend an hour in it before taking her final breath. We were not used to this. It was a new reality we had to deal with daily.

As I said before, we had no idea what we were dealing with at the time. Our safety was not everyone's top priority either. We were fighting a battle with no end date in sight.

There were no clear guidelines, and policies kept changing after every executive meeting. It was a race against time. The way we used to do things changed and we were quickly learning to adapt to the new rules.

Fear was raising its ugly head as we were not just losing patients but also colleagues. They were now contracting this very contagious and deadly virus and, instead of saving other people's lives, they were fighting to keep breathing, fighting to ensure that every breath they took would not be the last.

We were exhausted, frustrated, and afraid. We wore the crown of fear every day when we entered the hospital. Our red, tired eyes were bleeding dry as we comforted each other—burned out. The passion I once had for the job was fading. It was extinguished by exhaustion. We kept going trying our hardest to keep our heads above water. Our bones were trembling beneath the pressure, weakened by the daily 12-hour shifts. We kept moving because we had a job to do.

Each Thursday after work, it became a ritual for the people in the neighborhood to clap for us as we left the hospital. We were thankful and appreciated the gesture. However, this new clapping ritual could not bring joy back to our already crushed spirits. We lost the war against COVID-19 daily. The clappers saw us as heroes, but we saw ourselves as losers, defeated.

I know what defeat feels like but refuse to crumble under its weight. We could not allow others to see us defeated.

It was a good thing we were wearing those masks and face shields because they hid the tears and fear that covered our faces. No one saw them, but we knew they were there.

Covid was stealing the joy and harmony of every nurse, support worker, doctor, porter, and all the other hospital staff. We became experts at double masking; the invisible layer and the outer layer protected us from danger and our own vulnerability.

This war was fast and furious, claiming more lives than suicide bombers in the Middle East. I have been to war. In April

2004, I was a British soldier on a peacekeeping tour in Iraq, and the daily body count in the hospital from covid outnumbered those who died in that war. This mission was different, at least, you could hear the explosion; if you were lucky, you could see the traps and mine fields, as well as the enemy.

I was fighting a different war. This enemy could not be seen, heard, smelled, or touched. It was invisible, dangerous, and deadly.

If we are honest with ourselves, we would admit we live in fear of dying every day. Since covid made its grand entrance into this world, people are very fearful. We fear the uncertainty of who will be the next victim or statistic.

Many families are mad, angry, and upset at the world. Most of the time, they tend to take out their frustration on healthcare workers. Working in the field, we have become invisible to the human eye. We can go from superheroes to zero in a split second.

People never stop for a moment to realize that nurses carry many hats. We are caregivers, comforters, patient advocates, counselors, and more. Yet, our fears, anxiety, guilt, and a list of other emotions are unseen and unheard.

Honestly, with the pandemic, I had no idea what any given day would be like.

As I stepped through those doors of the main entrance of the hospital and walked down those long empty stretches of the hallway to commence my duty, I was forced to forget the pain of my life and robotically perform the duties ahead. We could not pause; we had to carry on. I know of those who did not get to bury their parents or be there with families because they were expected to get back to work as usual. Was that the new normal?

Several nurses had migrated from the Caribbean, India, Africa, and the Philippines to England to help reduce the shortage of nurses here. So when we received the news of our relatives dying in our homelands and we could not travel home because of the restrictions, it was devastating. We had to mourn alone in a faraway land without family and loved ones around us.

Many faced the silence of the night alone in a room without familiar faces in isolation. There were no social activities to engage in on your day off or after work as all the establishments were closed to the public.

It's sad to say that our feelings had to be set aside and then picked back up once we left the establishment. The elephant in the room was never addressed, and most times, nurses left their shifts without expressing how they really felt about losing patients they had created bonds with.

We bravely faced this pandemic and carried on as if nothing else mattered in the world than to keep those in our care alive. The challenges and struggles were too surreal to ignore. I listened to my colleagues express their fears with tears in their eyes while we raced against time to save both patients and co-workers. The fear in their eyes spoke volumes.

I was so exhausted and grounded in the routine of work that I forgot I was grieving the loss of my mother. She was the one I would call to offload and get some strong words of encouragement from. I was forced into a workaholic mood to suppress my emotions. Many times, after taking a tongue lashing from the relatives of someone who died, I wished the floor would open up and take me in. Sadly, we are often treated rudely and poorly whilst burning the candle at both ends.

People never stop for a moment to acknowledge we have real feelings and might have been sad or hurt by something that happened during a shift. And maybe we too are mourning a loss of some kind. When you take away the titles of nurse and health care professionals, we are human beings. We are mothers, daughters, sons, fathers, husbands, and wives. We hurt like everyone else.

People don't even stop to ask or consider we have feelings. We are hurt by their words and actions. Our day might not always be as bright as the smiles we fake or the sweet voices that echo in your ears.

If you were to ever strip us out of the uniform we wear, you would notice the bad, deep wounds underneath. The x-rays of us show we are broken, crushed, and ripped in many places.

We hid many tears because we were afraid people would consider us too weak for this job or that we were not cut out to be nurses. We worried they might say we were too in touch with our emotions. Many times, during my military training, I heard those words spoken by the trainers. They made silly comments and jokes indicating that showing emotions is a sign of weakness. Yet, one of our core values is compassion.

How can we live without emotions? They make us human. I learned the hard way our emotions don't make us weak. They help us deal with issues much better and break down barriers.

We battle with our anxiety to be present every day we enter the doors of the hospital we work at. The minute I enter those doors I transform into a different person. I can't talk about the sick child I left at home, the loss of the loved one I am grieving. It is totally out of character to walk into work worried about your own issues.

I walked around with a mask on my face hiding the pain, tears, sadness, and guilt I carried. In my distress, no one stopped, even for a moment to ask if my heart was okay. Sometimes I wondered if they saw me at all.

While I was at work every day from March until July during the time of my mother's death, it was hard, but I could not let it show. During those periods of isolation with nowhere to go other than walking back home, I often stopped to cry before I made it into the front door. I never wanted my daughter to see those hopeless tears and fear in my eyes.

Being in the hospital, I prayed the shift would end as quickly as it started because every time I lost a patient, I had to swallow the pain back into the pit of my stomach. My lips would tremble, and my voice would get hoarse, but there wasn't a safe space to express that.

My anxiety level would go from zero to one hundred in a split second. The staff toilet became my refuge where I escaped to let the warm string of tears kiss my face. There, I could be honest and vulnerable with myself. There, I could feel my heart restart as it beat again reminding me it would be okay. There, in the privacy of my own thoughts, no one disturbed my thinking as I allowed the light to crack through the darkness. There, I felt safe and protected.

I felt guilty because I know how much it hurts to learn your loved one has died, and you did not get to say goodbye. However, I still had to make those calls to inform relatives their loved ones passed away. I felt guilty because I couldn't ease their pain or take it away. However, I had to draw the line and not get too emotionally attached.

Losing a loved one is never easy. But the reality is in the midst of death, life persists. Therefore, we must find the strength and courage to carry on our everyday lives. Below are some suggestions to cope with grief on the job:

1. Step out of the situation for a while. Find a place where you can be vulnerable and cry. I used the bathroom.
2. Take self-care breaks, regroup and go back to work.
3. Listen to those around you and always give your co-workers a chance to vent.
4. Find your breathing space so you can carry on with the task ahead.
5. Care for others as you would yourself and family.
6. Remember it's okay not to be okay. We are human and grief affects us all, no matter the profession.
7. Talk about your own grief.
8. Don't bottle grief up; release it.
9. Accept that crying is not a sign of weakness; it is a source of strength. Therefore, weep if you must.
10. Breathe and let the pain out.

Chapter Takeaways

1. Despite your loss and grief, life inadvertently continues, and you must learn to navigate through your loss while still being present in the lives of others—on the job, at church, in your family, and community.

2. Look for a support group of persons who are familiar with grief and loss so that you can draw strength from each other.

3. Grief, loss, and tears may be hidden, but it is part of the journey. It is a phase of the process. Embrace that you are in that phase, but do not get stuck in it.

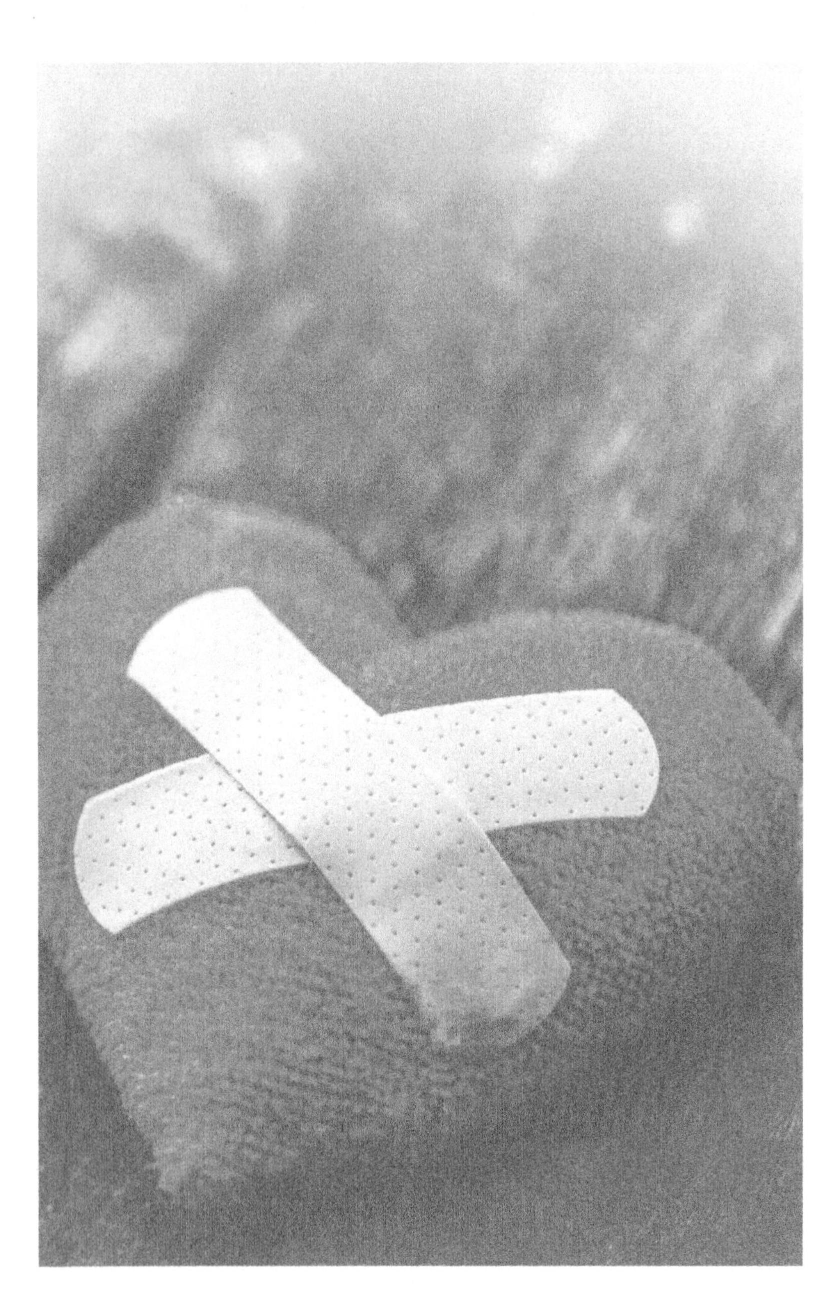

CHAPTER 5

Losing the Queen of Our Hearts

"Your life was a blessing, your memory a treasure.
You are loved beyond words and missed beyond measure."
— **RENEE WOOD**

I am still grieving the loss of my mother in the middle of the covid pandemic. I carried on despite my heartaches. My golden heart stopped beating while I carried on working. It was the best thing to do. It kept my mind off the problems. Life tossed me a lemon and I did not make lemonade. Rather, I ate it and tasted the bitterness.

It was a beautiful Sabbath day, March 21, 2020. My day began with me getting ready for church. I had a long refreshing shower that felt like the best I ever had. The water rolled down my golden-brown skin. It felt different.

When I finally carefully stepped out of the glass cubicle, I stopped briefly to admire my shadow in the bathroom mirror. I just had the feeling it would be a lovely day. Walking into my bedroom through the connecting door, I gently walked over to my dressing table and paused for a moment to choose from the selection of body lotion. Spoilt for choice, it took me a few minutes until I consciously agreed to soak my skin with a lovely scent of warm, vanilla sugar from the Bath and Body Works gifted to me by my dad.

My silk unstraightened jet black hair was gracefully brushed into an irresistible ponytail. Then I slowly applied some Vaseline to my lips to add some extra shine to them. To finish my appearance for the morning, I put on my navy-blue dress accompanied by a stunning pair of navy blue and black stilettos. I was all set, ready to greet them with my presence. Walking over to the corner where my iPad was, I took one more glance at myself in the mirror above the fireplace.

I slowly made my way to the grey corner sofa near the window in the sitting room. The light from the sunshine beamed into the room as it reflected on the well-polished floor. It was a beautiful spring morning.

I sat down to punch in the login details as today, it was nothing like the ordinary church. It was going to be the new way of doing things from now on as all the places of worship were closed. Schools and everywhere people gathered were closed. Isolation and social distancing were in full effect. No face-to-face contact was allowed.

No more stretched-out arms to give or receive a welcoming embrace followed by a quick conversation about how the weeks were. Church services were now virtual. People had to use their devices to attend. But there were more black screens than faces or pictures. Even the names they used to log in were unfamiliar. Though we congregated online, that warm, personal feeling we once had was gone. Who was iPad? Who was Samsung 109 or three heart emojis? Sometimes, we quickly learned who was behind the name when their faces appeared. But many times, we didn't.

"Welcome to our virtual service" was the greeting on the screen. "I know it is not our usual way of worship, but we thank God for taking us safely through another week. I also hope we have a blessed and wonderful day today."

It was a lovely service though different. After service, I had my lunch and then called my mother as I normally did.

"Hello!"

"Hello, Abney, where is Mommy? Can I talk to her?"

"Okay!" Abney replied and ran off shouting, "Mommy! Mommy! Auntie is on the phone."

"Good morning, Mommy. How are you?"

"I am fine! How are you, my daughter?" she asked.

"I am doing okay. I just finished church," I replied. "It was online, different but good."

As we continued our conversation, she jokingly asked me if I wanted lunch as she normally did. She said, "Today, I cooked sweet potatoes, yams, bananas, and fried fish."

"Yes, please," I said excitedly.

We spoke for a while and then she told me she had to go finish up her laundry. I promised to call her back later as it was only after 10 a.m. in St. Lucia. I was five hours ahead in England. I put the phone down and had an afternoon nap, hoping to call my mom later.

There was no evening service, so when I got up from my nap, I had dinner with my daughter. After dinner, we went into the living room where I made a few phone calls to friends. The evening was going fine. My daughter and I planned our lunch menu for the following day, which also happened to be my day off. With the shops closed, we decided to spend the day indoors watching a movie or something. There wasn't much to do as we were in isolation and could not meet anyone outside our household.

My daughter and I sat on the sofa talking as we waited to join our family in St. Lucia for our 6 p.m. family worship session. That was something we did every evening. However, when the phone rang, it wasn't for family worship; it was something else. At first, when my sister called, I thought she was doing so for my mother to start our devotions. But I was so wrong.

That evening, my sister told me Mom had fallen sick while on the road. What? When I spoke to her that morning, she was fine. I panicked. My heart started racing. Sweat rolled down my back. My heart pounded as if it was about to explode. But somehow, I found the strength to type a message to my church group asking them to pray for my mother.

Not having many details of what actually happened, a lot was playing on my mind. A million questions raced through my head. Did she get hit? Did she miss her footing? Did she suffer a seizure? What happened to her? How long was she there before someone found her?

I rang my sister back trying to get more information about what was really going on. At that time, they were waiting for the ambulance to arrive. I called Rafati and explained to him what had happened. He rushed to where my mother was before the ambulance got there and took Mom to the hospital. My sister and uncle accompanied her.

She made it to the hospital, but it was too late. My phone rang and instantly, I knew it wasn't good news. The screams in the background said it all.

"Jay, your mother did not make it."

"They killed my mother!" I shouted in despair.

"First they killed my sister and now my mother!" I screamed.

I had to find someone to blame. Still in shock and denial, I believed the medical staff did not do all they could to save my mother and sister.

Those familiar emotions swept over me, the same ones I felt when I lost my sister. Guilt returned. Would they have died if I was there? I would have known what to do. I could have done CPR and put her in the recovery position. I do this every day. I do everything within my capacity to keep my patients alive, but now, I was too far away to be of any help to the ones closest and dearest to my heart.

I was helpless.

I felt as if a hand was choking me, cutting off my oxygen supply. I had witnessed people rolling on the floor in grief and never thought I would do it. But I was on my knees, screaming, crying, and angry at everything and everyone.

Some of our church family who lived close by broke protocol and came over to be with us. They stayed with us for roughly an hour encouraging us as best as they could and then left.

Lies and Childhood Sorrow

I could not eat, sleep, or stop crying. As the days went by, I got messages from different church members, families, friends, and Facebook friends with words of encouragement and support. Most of the messages were encouraging except one. It came in the form of a voice note telling me I needed to pray because there was a spiritual reason my family members were dying within a short period of each other.

Those words were like a stab in the back. Painful. In difficult situations, my grandmother used to say if you cut her open, you would not see any blood. I felt like that.

I could not even pray for myself much less pray against spiritual attacks on my family. Honestly, that wasn't a thought that ever crossed my mind. But I was at my lowest and Satan made me believe it was true, that my family was indeed cursed, and I was being punished.

All the negative things that were said about my family years before when I was growing up returned to my memory. Instantly, I believed they were true and that was the reason for all those sudden deaths. Once again, I was reliving my childhood that I wanted

to leave buried in the past. Let's just say things that were being said about my family at that time were too painful and associated with a lot of negativities. Growing up in the community, I was often ridiculed by community members and their children. In today's society, we call it bullying.

It was painful and scary, but it needed to be addressed to heal. It was rumored that my grandfather was my biological father, which was far from the truth.

I was in Grade 6 at the time when I had a bitter misunderstanding with another student that led to an exchange of words. During that altercation, she said her mother told them that my grandfather was having children with his daughters.

I thought that was a bit strange of her to say since my grandfather also had children with her grandmother. Therefore, that too would make her my grandfather's daughter. This was my first and last fight at school and my teachers were very disappointed with me. I was one of the star athletes at both primary and secondary schools and they expected better.

Arriving at school, I had to explain to my mother why the golden chain with the heart-shaped picture pendant was missing. I got the disappointed mother's look with a telling off that she did not send me to school to be a fighter. However, before my mother could finish her statement, my aunty came to my rescue and said, "The child needs to stand up for herself."

"People will always say things that are not true, but it doesn't mean she has to defend herself against such. They will come to their conclusions about your situations," my mother would say.

Ours was a community where everyone knew everybody's business. Whether it was true or not, it would spread like wildfire. It took me a while, but I learned quickly that no matter how much you try to explain the truth, people only believe their versions of the story.

As I mentioned in the previous chapter, my dad left St. Lucia after high school and wasn't around during my childhood. Hence, not many people knew he was my father.

Mommy was always the peacekeeper in the family—the "soft one" they called her.

I knew the truth about our grandmother's father because we always visited him with her on Sunday afternoons. My great-granddad was a fisherman, and we would often go to the beach with granny to collect fish from him. I enjoyed going to the beach as a child because he always had sweets and other goodies for us when we got there.

As I mentioned previously, when my mother passed, the boundaries were closed due to the pandemic. Most countries were urging their nationals to return home on the next available flights, and repatriation flights were arranged to get nationals back to their home countries.

All air and sea travel came abruptly to a standstill. Only essential traveling was advised. Airlines canceled all flights and vacation was no more. I searched the Internet hoping something would come up somewhere out of the blue.

Virgin Atlantic and British Airways' apps and customer services were my best friends. I called and searched relentlessly, only to hear, "Sorry, we don't know when flights will be resuming. I even tried the high commissioner's office in London but did not qualify as a returning national; therefore, they could not help me get home. I wanted to be in St. Lucia in our family home—anywhere but not here in England.

In my desperation, I tried searching for other routes to get home but to no avail. Every avenue I tried was a dead end. I could not even set a date to travel from England to St. Lucia. But I had faith and a sense of hope that I would get to travel to bury my mother.

Being my mother's firstborn and eldest daughter, I was the main source of income. My sister could not make any decisions without my consent. I was the next of kin and the one with power of attorney.

My mother had me at the tender age of 15 years and was the single parent of five children and grandmother of five. Mommy was our best friend, and she loved us unconditionally. She was my world.

She sacrificed everything to make me who I am today as a single mother working for five dollars a day in a factory. Before working in the factory, she worked as a housekeeper in a hotel until it closed: Sadoo Restaurant and LA Foods. She did odd jobs like cleaning and ironing for people to make ends meet.

She worked in the factory for 17 years and used to sell jam, breadsticks, and many other things to provide for her children. This woman I knew for 39 years of my life did not say goodbye to me, and I hated that fact. I spoke to her in the morning and there was no sign it would have been the last conversation.

I often wonder if I would ever be half the mother she was to us. She was a jar full of love overflowing into others. Hardly can I recall a moment when this woman failed to help others. Our home was forever a full house where strangers could sleep, eat, and stay as long as they wanted.

She wasn't just our mother but a mother to every child who needed a mother's love. She raised more children than she gave birth to, and we never had to compete for her love and affection as she never showed favoritism. If she ever did have a favorite child, sibling, niece, or nephew, that was a secret she took to her grave.

The glue that kept the family together was my mom. Mommy was more than a grandmother to my daughter, nieces, and nephew. She took them everywhere she went. No one was left behind when she went to church on Sundays.

My mother was my first best friend, my number one fan, and my support. She was my role model, adviser, and prayer warrior. She was our very own doctor when we were ill. She filled up every ounce of my heart. Words fail me when it comes to conveying how much my mother meant to me and my siblings.

The sound of gospel music always soothes my heart as it reminds me of my mother's music playing at full volume accompanied by her singing at the top of her voice. Most of the time, she would make the words up as she sang along. Indeed, she knew how to carry her own key and that's something I will forever cherish. It brings tears to my eyes, but I smile through them because, at times, I would find myself singing my mother's version of the songs.

Mom was always in communication with God, even on the day she died. He was the last person she spoke to. If you ever needed my mother on a Wednesday, you were most certain to find her in the church for their regular prayer, fasting, and anointing service. The love she had for God could not be replaced, and she did not take that aspect of her life lightly.

Mom constantly reminded us that she was here to do God's business and this world has nothing to offer her. She encouraged us and others to take that aspect of our lives seriously.

"Don't joke with God," she would warn us.

"If you are not serious, don't go out playing church."

She prayed for us without ceasing. I can still feel that drop of olive oil rolling down my nose from the tip of my big forehead where she placed her hand and committed me and my siblings to God in prayer.

She had a daily appointment with God from 2 a.m. I could not escape it when I was on the island for holiday. At times, I thought my mom was disturbing my sleep. Why couldn't she wait until morning? I wasn't brave enough to ask her that. After all, it was her time with God. And just imagine; four hours later, she would be up doing her prayer walk in the house. Afterward, that delicious aroma would fill the house with her cooking, still praying, and talking to God.

I would go into my sister's room and whisper, "Your mother doesn't sleep."

She would say, "You only have to put up with it for a few weeks. We have to all year round."

Now, I find myself doing the same thing from time to time, waking up at odd hours of the night praying for comfort and strength to carry on and be there for my siblings, daughter, nieces, and nephews.

Mom would be the first person at the hospital when she found out a family member or a friend was there. Yes, you guessed it; she would be praying there as well.

When my best friend had surgery, my mother went to visit her at home and took my niece along with her. If my memory serves me correctly, my niece was only two years old, and she too was anointing my friend and praying for her.

My friend said, "Jay your mother taught Abney well. At that age, she already knows how to pray. I was touched and moved by the prayers."

Mother put prayer first in everything, and she did not just believe, but she also knew that God would answer in His timing. For that reason, whenever I was having personal issues, she was the first person I would pour out my heart to. Instantly, she would lift me to God in prayer.

I received many answers to prayer when my mother prayed for me. I miss our bond. And for such reason, I was mad at God and asked Him how He could cut my mother's life short. How could He do this to us again? For a second time, He took the thread that was holding our hearts together.

I wasn't too sure whether I was mad at God for allowing the pandemic that prevented me from being able to travel as soon as I received the news of my mother's passing or for my reasons. Whichever it was, I was mad, and God took the blame.

I just wanted to be home at that point with my family, but I could not travel. It was a distant but ever-constant thought. I allowed myself to be positive when talking to others. I spoke believing God would come through at the right time.

I remember clearly telling my grandmother that they should not even bury my mother without me there. Burying my mother created a lot of pressure because she died at the beginning of the covid pandemic and there was nothing I could do.

I used to get very angry when people asked when the burial was because they knew it was a gamble. I honestly had no idea whether I would be able to travel that year or not, but I kept hope alive.

I managed to make all the funeral arrangements whilst still in lockdown in the UK with faith and hope that the boundaries would open in time for me to say farewell to my mother.

We eventually left for St. Lucia on July 26, 2020, which wasn't the original date. We were meant to travel on the 25th but received an email stating that due to a storm expected to hit the island, the flight would be the following day. However, before traveling, we had to take the PCR tests and upload the results on the National Health Service app.

We had to apply for government quarantine in St. Lucia as all visitors or returning nationals were required to do before travel. It was a new way of traveling but I had to do it because I wanted to be home. All the protocols were followed, and my checklist ticked, ready for our 8-hour flight. Not forgetting our masks and extra to change during the flight.

God allowed my travel to be delayed but that delay placed me in a better financial position. I was able to top up my bank account. As soon as I got to St. Lucia, I received an email from the airline company informing me that our return journey was canceled, and we needed to rebook. I couldn't secure a date until November.

My daughter and I had to spend 14 days in quarantine—ten at a government-assigned hotel and the other four at home. We were at home but still ten days away from our family and friends. My brother and Dayna brought us water and juice for our stay in quarantine. We did not get to see them as they were only allowed to drop off the stuff at the gate.

Every single morning and night, the nurses did our temperature checks, and, on the eighth day, we had to repeat the covid tests. If they were negative, we would go home. Our results were negative. I could not wait to get out of there.

Being in the house was the hardest day of my life. When I looked at the stove, tears welled up in my eyes because the kitchen was where you would find my mom. She loved cooking and her food was the best.

I tried avoiding the places in the house that reminded me of her, and the void was killing me. Many times, the tears came. But I quickly wiped them away since Grandma was staying with us. I had to put on a brave face for her. The few times I caught her crying broke my heart, but I could not join in. I did not want to make things worse for her and the kids.

I kept myself busy with the funeral arrangements to blank out the fact that I was grieving and hurt. I believe the three-week-old baby my mom adopted from the hospital helped to distract me. Looking after her kept my mind off the real reason I was in St. Lucia.

The day of the burial came, and I did the eulogy. I don't know where I got the courage, but I did. God knows I was bleeding inside. The pastor even commented on it. He reminded everyone present that it was love and we will see our mother again if we are faithful and follow the path she has paved for us.

Truthfully, I seemed fine on the outside but inside, I was hurting. I was struggling with the fact that today was the final day of my mother's earthly presence. Physically, I was present but invisible emotionally. I had to show up for my siblings, especially my baby sister, my nieces, nephew, and disabled brother who thought they could look after themselves.

My niece had to face such an ordeal twice, first her mother and now, her grandmother who practically raised her.

On August 15, 2020, I made the hardest decision of all: learning to let go of my mother's presence on the earth. Many of the well-wishers came to me to express how blessed they were to have met my mother. She was never short of an encouraging word and a prayer. They said, "Hold on to that." It's been over a year, almost two, and people are still messaging me to remind me of the wonderful woman my mother was. She left her imprint, not only on us but also on others she met.

To My Dearest Mother

As the years moved on, I waited in great anticipation for what my heart would feel.

The anxiety of this day plays with the strings of my heart, and the melody is neither sweet nor sour.

As the tears stream, they burn my face with their warmth.

My lips tremble in the silence as my mind thinks aloud, mother. Oh, mother, I miss you.

It's two years now, mummy, and my heart is pumping in pain.

Time has again made a mockery of me because to think of the love that is missing, time can never heal.

It hurts cause I miss you. It hurts because your humble heart and gentle smile have gone. It hurt just because today is the 21st of March.

A day forever pencilled in the diary of my mind. I miss you, my dearest mother. Love you always.

Continue to rest in perfect peace.

Chapter Takeaways

1. Take every opportunity to speak with loved ones (even when living abroad). You truly never know when they will pass on.

2. When someone is mourning or grieving the loss of a loved one, words matter. Many are overzealous to give words of comfort during that time, but sometimes, saying less and being more present is far more than a word spoken out of turn.

3. During grief, sharing how the lost loved one touched your life may greatly encourage the grieving family. They will appreciate that their loved one meant something to others outside of themselves and realize that their loss is the loss of community members.

4. Feeling helpless during times of loss and mourning is almost natural, especially if you are the "backbone" of your family. Understand that everything is in God's hands and not yours.

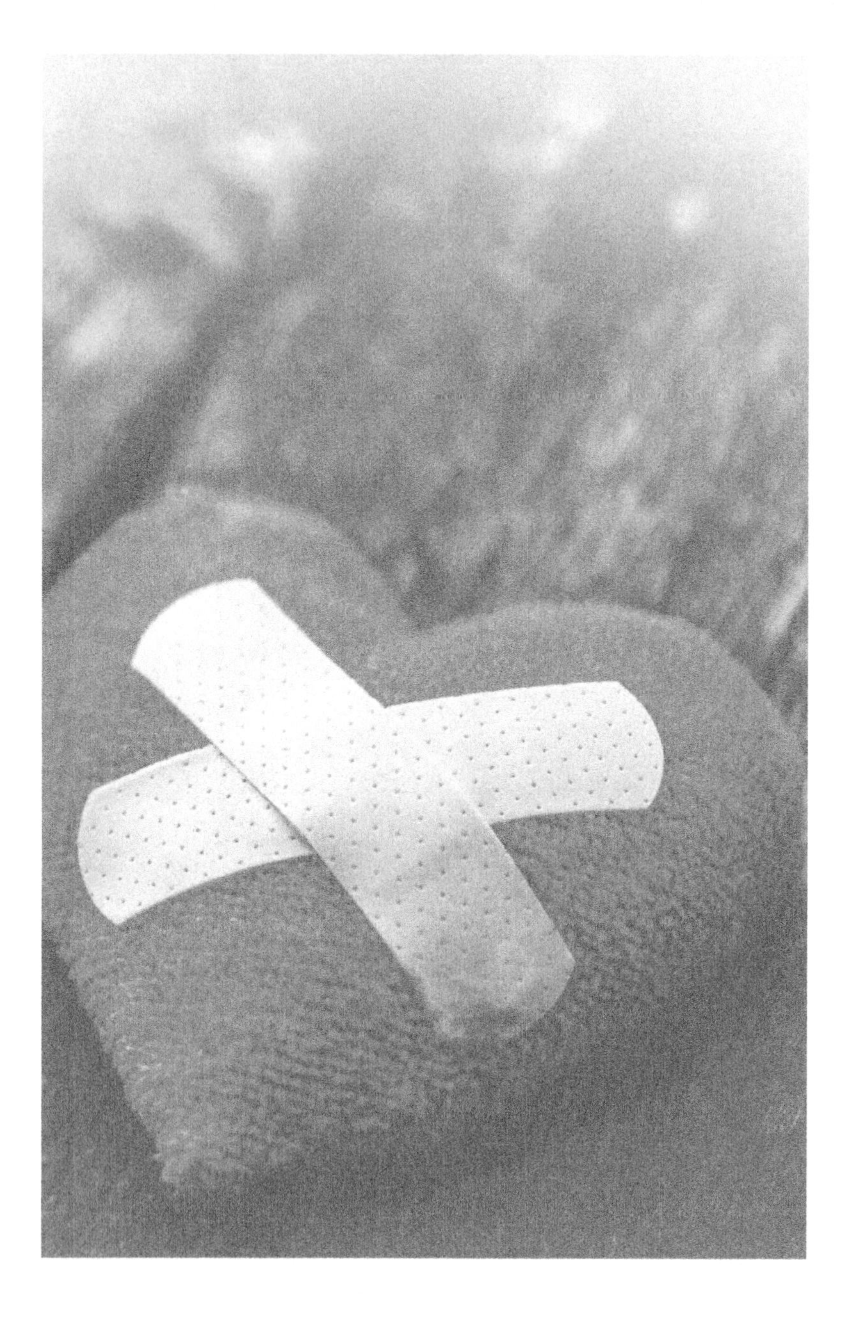

Chapter 6

Death Is a Natural Part of Life

"It is as natural to die as it is to be born."
—FRANCIS BACON

On my first day as a student nurse, I experienced my very first face-to-face encounter with death. I wasn't ready. What started as a very exciting day for me, quickly turned gloomy. The reality hit me that it was not all sunshine. It wasn't all about the glorious moments when we save someone's life.

That day, I saw death's remorseless eyes. They were fixed on a ninety-six-year-old lady, lying comfortably between the crisp white sheets of a freshly made-up bed, in a six-bed bay at a large university teaching hospital.

I was a very excited and eager student nurse ready to learn the practical side of my career. As part of our training, we had to do placements alongside our theory. Facing the reality of the job is what my mentor called it.

The week before, I had rushed to the notice board at the university faculty office and anxiously pushed my way through to the front, along with my friend. My heart danced with joy when I realized I got my placement of choice. I was excited about this for many reasons but mainly because it was a ten-minute walk from home. It was the ideal choice, I did not have to take the bus or train, just a walk up the road. I was the envy of some of my peers. "You are very lucky your placement is just at your doorstep they would remind me."

I got to sleep for an extra hour and returned home much earlier, especially during the winter when it gets dark at 3 p.m.

The day of my placement arrived, and I was up before my alarm went off. I was too anxious to sleep, so instead, I kept waking up every hour. I decided to get ready since I was already up. My uniform was ironed the night before, so I packed my bag with my lunch and water bottle.

Then I took a shower, combed my relaxed hair into a ponytail, took care to put on my well-ironed hospital blue stripe with white trim around the collar and pockets, and my navy-blue trousers. On my feet, I wore a brand-new pair of black Puma trainers.

My student ID badge was on my bottom pocket and a black pen and a red pen in my top right pocket with a fob watch pinned on the outside. All set and ready, I left the house half an hour earlier than I had originally planned.

I walked the street already flooded with a busy flow of cars and red double-decker buses as pedestrians negotiated and hurried along. People were hopping on and off the buses going about their business.

It was a typical early morning in the United Kingdom. The skies were dark although it was 6:30 a.m. The long stretch of road was illuminated by the flooded streetlights and oncoming vehicles.

The sound of footsteps could be heard moving quickly to catch the bus before it took off. I was glad I only had to walk a few blocks before I reached the hospital. I climbed a few steps, maybe four or five, and then carefully made my way through the rotating glass door. I headed straight to the sign that read "Main Reception."

"Good morning! I am a first-year nursing student, and I am looking for the medical assessment unit," I said to the lady at the desk.

She gave me the information I needed and wished me all the best for the day. However, in that big hospital, I got lost along the way and had to ask a lady dressed in a dark blue uniform for directions. She was the head of nursing and in charge of the students. I found that out after she welcomed me and pointed me to the ward that was not too far away.

I arrived on the ward and reported to the nurse in charge. She pointed to a room and asked me to drop my bag and coat then follow her. I followed her into a large room that looked like a meeting room but just smaller. I learned later that it was the handover room. The nurse in charge quickly checked a folder in her hand after I told her who I was.

She replied, "I am expecting you and three other students." I was early, so I sat in a quiet room waiting for the others to arrive. While waiting, I scanned the room and noticed lots of works of literature and articles on the walls and bulletin boards. Some of those articles and posters were the hospital's policies and guidelines, which did not take us long to learn and memorize.

Finally, the others arrived, and the night nurses gave the handover. However, I was lost most of the time by the abbreviations used. I was allocated a mentor, and she gave me a handbook with all the abbreviations. In my own time, I became familiar with them, and they are now a part of my regular conversations and documentation.

This was my first placement and as first-year students, we were only allowed to do the basics without supervision. This involved making the beds, assisting with feeding but not those patients at risk of choking, assisting with a bed, bath, shower, etc.

As the day progressed, I met a ninety-six-year-old lady completely bed-bound and sweet in nature.

"Hello, my name is Jermila. I am a student nurse, and I am looking after you today together with my mentor."

"Nice to meet you. What a pretty name," she said.

"Thank you, I've been told my name means beautiful in Arabic."

"It sure does. Ain't you a pretty little thing?" she said in her soft British accent.

"Thank you," I responded with a smile on my face.

Continuing our conversation, I said, "If there's anything else you need, please let us know by squeezing the orange button." I placed the call bell on the table within her reach.

"Sure," she replied.

"Can you give me a drop of water? My mouth is on fire."

I proceeded with the request and gave her a drink of water. However, instead of using the call bell, she kept calling out for more water when the jug of water was empty.

It was as if in the flash of a moment as I turned my back to refill her jug of water that I heard an unfamiliar sound. I turned toward the staff in the kitchen who reminded me that it was an emergency call.

With the empty jug in hand, I ran toward the sound of the buzzer when I noticed everyone else was heading in the same direction as me: toward the old lady's bedside. Only a moment ago she was fine.

Staff ran from all directions, and the ward sister signaled to me to bring the resuscitation trolley. I immediately unplugged the trolley from the wall and pushed it toward the room.

The resuscitation trolley contains equipment that helps to restart someone's heart in the event of cardiac arrest. As standard practice, this trolley is checked at the end of every night shift roughly around 6 a.m. daily, replacing any missing items, expired equipment, and medications.

As I approached the room with the trolley, the doctor announced, "She is gone."

"What do you mean she's gone? No, she can't be," I mumbled. "We were just having a conversation a few minutes ago, so she can't be gone. She was perfectly okay when I left her side."

At this point, I was having a one-way communication as no one answered my questions. In a room full of people, not one person acknowledged hearing what I was asking.

I had just left her to fill up her jug with more water. The last thing she said to me was "Can I have a drop of water?"

Looking in the direction of the bed, I saw her lifeless body. Her face was as pale as the white, cotton sheets. She just lay there peacefully and motionless. Registering the shock and disbelief on my face, the ward sister took me aside and said, "You can finish early today. I think that is enough for the first day."

I could not read her emotions, or she was so used to it that she knew how to hide or disconnect from them. As I matured in the profession, like her, I learned when to disconnect myself and emotions from those moments that could break you.

I could have chosen to end this career here, but I didn't. As I transitioned from a student nurse to a staff nurse. Death became a part of my day-to-day life. I cared for many patients at the end of their lives.

How quickly death appears was never quite explained in length or detail. Knowing it will happen is one thing but how and when are something else. They were totally different. No amount of reading or knowledge can ever prepare you for that face-to-face encounter with death.

The critical lesson I learned on my first day on placement was death is a natural part of life. Dying is a part of living; it is an active process we will all go through someday. Yet, death is like a mystery. It can feel like turning the pages of a novel with no words or story, unable to know what happens next, and that can be very scary.

As much as we know that death is a natural part of life when it happens, it still comes with an element of surprise.

My Greatest Fears about Death

In talking to friends, colleagues, and family members, I found something very interesting. Many of us are not afraid of death. It is not knowing when it will happen that frightens us. We are afraid of the feelings and emotions associated with death.

The death of a human being is considered a sad or unpleasant occasion due to the love for the deceased and the cessation of the social bond. Death is never referred to as a joyous moment. It is sad, whether we know the person or not. Just knowing the person is no longer here is heart-breaking.

If I am honest with myself, at times, I fear not being able to accomplish my bucket list or having enough time with those I love. I am afraid that someday, I will not be able to smile and laugh so hard that my jawbones hurt.

The countless phone calls to my loved ones will end. My seat at the family table will be empty. A day will come when those warm embraces and shoulders to cry on will no longer be available. I am afraid that someday, I might not make it home after work or a casual walk. I worry that I will not feel the warmth of the sun and cold of the winter on my skin or the water or sweat rolling down my flesh. I will not hear, smell, or see the things that once surrounded me—a busy street or the smell of pollution in the air.

The noise that once stole my peace will all be gone someday.

I fear not seeing my nieces and nephew grow, what will happen to those around me, their progress in life, and their accomplishments.

I wonder about what will be the last thing I eat, the last place I visit, and the last person to call my name. There will be no more welcome at the door and no one will call your sweet name. Those are the things I fear most when the random thought of death comes to my subconscious.

What Do You Fear about Death?

Morbid as it may seem, sometimes pinpointing your fears about death can be therapeutic. Have you ever been honest about that area of your life? Have you thought about your immortality? It may help you face the painful reality that your loved one has crossed a bridge that one day you too will go. Take a few minutes to look within. Ask yourself these questions and write the answers down. They will help you express your true feelings, process them, and examine your fears.

1. Are you afraid of death?

2. What exactly is it about death that scares you?

3. Are your fears based on fact or fiction? Are they realistic or based on what you imagine?

4. How is the fear of death affecting the way you live now?

Living in the Here and Now

"Our mortality and finitude remind us of the urgency of living here and now, with full engagement in life and with dedication to those around us. When death comes for us, let it find us among the living."

—IRVIN YALOM

It is amazing how living on the edge of life does not frighten me. I enjoy those long-haul flights over the ocean despite numerous reports of plane crashes. If you are like me, that's when I have the most peaceful sleep, not even an encounter with turbulence disturbs me.

During my first week in the army, we had two weeks of adventure training. I did things I never did before, including the very things my mom and family members considered risky. But I did them anyway. I took the plunge. I was young, full of adrenaline, and living by the motto: "I only live once."

I did things I could tell my children about and enjoyed capturing the moment on my disposable Kodak camera. Going through my mother's photo album, I could see how dangerous my adventures were—zipping from one end of the building to another and feeling the thrill it gave me. Many things could have gone wrong. The zip wire could have broken, and I could have fallen several feet to my death, but that did not cross my thoughts at the time. I experienced bungee jumping, white water rafting, even though I could not swim properly, canoeing dressed up in my wetsuit, rock climbing, pool driving, and mountain biking. On reflection, I realize any of those could have been fatal. But at the time, I was fearless and purely brave. My blood rushed with excitement as my colleagues cheered me on.

After all, I was training to be a soldier. I had to be brave or else, what use would I be in the army? I signed up for it. That's what I was often reminded of by those in charge.

I saw others overcome their fear of height, learn to ride, and drive, especially those HGV trailers. We conquered the impossible by doing things to give us purpose in life. We were living, not worrying about the inevitable—death.

Death and Spiritual Attacks

Death doesn't seem to be a problem until we encounter it unexpectedly or a family member calls to say he/she is critically ill to the point of dying. That's when we acknowledge it, and it pulls us down to our knees.

Growing up, to describe death, we would often say the person has gone to sleep. I was too young to understand when my uncle suddenly died. They just told me he had gone to sleep and would not be back for a very long time. They told me I would see him again when the world came to an end.

I was confused about death growing up. I believed my mother would always be around. If she got sick, she would get better. I thought my siblings and I would be around forever, doing many things together until we got old. I never thought they would die, at least, not before the age of 90 years old.

As I grew, I realized where there is life, there must be death. In fact, death and life go hand in hand. None exist without the other. Death is a natural cycle for all living things. Everything and everyone lives and dies.

Though death is a natural part of life, it seems to be something that none of us will ever come to terms with although unconsciously, we know it will happen to every one of us; it is just a matter of time or when. When it happens, to accept it, we enter a state of denial.

As I grieved the loss of my mother, sister, and uncle, just to mention a few, I was placed in a position where I questioned the nature of death because of a comment by a well-wisher.

Being at my lowest mentally and emotionally, I used the statement to justify my loss, and everything I knew as a nurse for over nine years became irrelevant. I have cared for countless dying patients, and I know full well that nothing or no one can escape death when the time comes. Life starts with one grand breath, and it ends in the same manner.

On many shifts, I've seen patients take their final breath as they inhale and exhale life. I've had the privilege to witness their color leaving their faces and changing from bright pink to pale in an instant. Sometimes, it happened so quickly you didn't even notice.

Although from experience, I know death is natural, I still questioned it looking for answers, trying to find a reason why so many of my loved ones were dying. It is easier to accept the fact that something is responsible for death when you are in my position. Knowledge becomes irrelevant. Grief can impact our mental state and cause us to be very confused.

I stood in that tunnel where I was searching for a crack of light to penetrate the darkness. Yet, a simple comment sent me down a spiral looking for an answer within the walls of my mind. I stopped for a minute and believed it was true.

I felt a blunt blow of the comment, and it stabbed me in my back like a piercing sword.

Every time I listened to the voice note, I felt the blood rushing from my head to my toes, saturating me with anger. I was angry at her too. How dare she suggest something like this. To add insult to injury, she followed her voice note with literature. I hardly spoke to this lady, and she knew nothing about my family and me. Yet, she messaged me with such foolishness, and I believed her.

Another statement many church folks made was, "Don't you think this could be a spiritual attack or something in your family causing the death of your loved ones? The first time I just brushed it aside but, after hearing it again, I was upset.

The statement forced me to examine my family and my life in search of the answer to something natural. At that point, I was convinced something had to be wrong. Some kind of generational curse was in my family, or I was doing something wrong so God was punishing me.

Being a Seventh Day Adventist, I was looking for what my shortcomings were. I joined the Adventist faith in 2008, after leaving the military. I got baptized on October 4, 2009, alongside a friend I met in basic training.

My mom was ecstatic when I told her the news that I was getting baptized. Her prayers were answered and now, I was walking with God. From that moment, I became very involved in the church and its activities.

I believed I was not following God as I should; therefore, He was punishing me with the death of so many family members. Honestly, despite the many offices I held in the church and studying the Bible, I was convinced God was not pleased about something in my life. My anger and self-condemnation caused me to drift from Him.

I was trapped in a minefield battle with God. We wrestled day and night. My faith was sliding away. It was easy to try to find my way back when my sister died because my mother was praying for us and encouraging us along the journey. She was the glue that held us together but when she died, the ship sank. I drifted further and further into the depth of the ocean. The anchor that was holding the ship together got broken and I lost my way. My compass was broken, and I could not navigate my way back. In my mind, I was alone, trying to find my way to dry land. I was lost.

I was present and very active at church, but I was going through the motion, putting on a show, and the audience was myself. I thought others were being blessed and encouraged by my service, but I wasn't sure I even believed the stuff I was saying. I was too far gone, and help could not be found.

The good news is that God is not like us, and He doesn't punish us in the way we think He will. He is compassionate and always near to the broken-hearted. When you lose your connection with Christ, doubt starts to set in. It even makes you question the truth. All of a sudden, what is right seems wrong and you find reasons to justify or validate what others say. However, peace and joy come when God helps you navigate your way back to Him.

Various cultures have different views about death and so do religions. We all have different ideologies and perspectives when such events occur, especially when they are closely related. Thus, we mourn differently. How we remember the dead is often influenced by our religious backgrounds and cultures.

I am very privileged to work with people from diverse backgrounds and religions. I have had discussions with a few of them about how they view death. As a nurse, I care for people from every walk of life. On one occasion, when a Muslim patient in my care died, I recalled that the family wanted his body released to them as soon as possible.

A doctor colleague of mine told me that when a Muslim dies, the corpse is treated with great respect. She also went on to say that the body continues to exist in the afterlife. Prayers are offered up daily for the dead and ideally, the burial should take place before 2 p.m. Embalming and cremation are not permitted. The only time an autopsy is permitted is for medical or legal reasons. Hence, the body must be released immediately to the family for burial—on the same day if possible. The dead person is remembered daily through prayers.

In the Hindu ritual, during the period of mourning, the family displays a picture of the dead, and mourning can happen for 10 to 30 days. During that time, mourners recite prayers to honor the dead. I was also told that cremation happens quickly, and family and friends often visit the house to offer sympathy. There are many branches of Hinduism and funeral rituals vary.

Growing up in the Caribbean, I remember when it was considered disrespectful to wear any other color to a funeral than black, white, purple, or a combination of those colors. There was something called "Nine Nights" where people in the community came together to support the family during this time. The tradition of having a wake is still around today but the dress code for the service has changed. These days, you can wear a touch of color in your attire to attend funerals.

There are many different religions in the Caribbean. Catholic is the religion of choice for many, and, during the burial service, there are lots of signs and prayers for the family and the dead. They also believe in the afterlife. Catholics have services such as mass that are held for the dead.

As Adventists, we believe death is a state of unconscious sleep until the resurrection. Our belief is based on biblical truth. Other Christian religions also hold the same view as us. The Bible states the dead are in a deep sleep waiting on Christ's second coming. We grieve because we miss our loved ones. Death will always be an unavoidable, inescapable, and undeniable fact of life.

We are well-prepared for life but not for death. We put all the planning in place to welcome a new life into the world, from choosing the outfits to the selection of names and gender reveals. Oh, what a joy just seeing those endless smiles on the mother and father's faces.

For some, the harsh reality of death comes creeping in even before life begins. That mother, wife, or girlfriend going through the stages of pregnancy only to miscarry days before the due date. That was the death of a baby who never got to say hello to his or her parents. Some spend a week and then say goodbye. These are the hardest moments that can never be explained.

My brother Jerson was a still birth. I never really got to see him because I was too young to go to the hospital with my mother at the time. It was late that night when my aunt took my mother to the hospital. I was excited the next morning when my grandmother told me Mom went to have the baby. Two to three days later, my mother returned home, but she did not have the baby. He died and was buried at the hospital grounds.

Life ends before it begins when babies die. It is a solemn reminder that death happens at any time during our life span, and it can cause a great deal of pain for those left in its path. Not only do babies die at birth but mothers also die during childbirth.

It is estimated that 830 women die from pregnancy-related causes every day according to the latest UN global estimates.

I had a friend who died hours after giving birth to her baby. Can you believe after years and years of miscarriages she was finally going to be a mother, but she never got to hold her baby and look her in the eye with love and compassion? Despite all the planning to welcome her baby into the world, she did not get to tell her how precious and special she was after many failed pregnancies.

In the medical field, we use the term "save a life" when in fact, we don't save lives; we just prolong them by using the best medicines and state-of-the-art equipment.

I say that because, while working in elderly care at the hospital, I have seen patients treated for a disease, only to return a few years later to die.

We do everything within our reach to prolong our lives. We change the way we eat, ensure we get enough sleep, exercise, rest, and get sunlight to live longer and healthier lives.

Are we afraid of dying or are we afraid of not being able to accomplish our goals in life?

You may be considering doing so much. Don't let it be a wish if you can do it. We are not guaranteed life beyond tomorrow. The mere fact that we are breathing qualifies us for death.

Why do we find it so difficult to normalize death? A ComRes survey from 2014, found that eight in ten Brits are uncomfortable talking about death and only a third have a written will. Death anxiety appears to be at the core of mental health disorders, and depressive disorders, and yet we are too scared to talk about it.

Being a professional in the field, I don't just randomly speak about death with my family. I don't just walk through the door and say, "Wow, I had an awful shift today because my patients died." I don't talk about it because I believe I am protecting them from it. I don't tell them how badly it hurts when you lose someone you care for daily.

How could I tell my family about it when there was a lack of fundamental education on death and dying apart from one session on breaking bad news. Yet, as soon as I qualified, I was expected to talk to patients and families about death and dying. What I am saying is we need to be more open about death. More education is needed in the profession I am in as we face this daily.

Why don't we prepare the younger generation for the inevitable?

There needs to be a safe space to properly educate our children, grandchildren, daughters, sisters, and sons, about our experiences dealing with death. It is a natural part of life. We can't outgrow or escape it.

How many of us put plans in place so when the day comes, our loved ones know what we want on our funeral day, instead of them guessing?

As I qualified and registered as a nurse, I secured a job in my local hospital caring for the elderly on a medical ward. Part of my duty is the documentation, filling in the admission paperwork to create a care plan for our patients. One of the sections deals with end-of-life care, covering what the patients would like done if they die while in hospital.

Their spiritual preferences and their last wishes were among the sections that needed to be filled. Most times, we try to honor the wishes of the dying, but the conflict comes when we realize that this was never a conversation they had with the family. For example, a person may wish to die in hospital, but the family believes he would be better dying at home.

I notice I never had those conversations with my loved ones. I never asked them about their end-of-life wishes or informed them of mine. I thought it was too early, but I was too late and never had a conversation with my mother or sister. Their deaths happened too fast and way too early.

Due to modern technology and the advancement in medicine, people are now aware of how long they have before dying from certain illnesses. Science has allowed for the prolonging of life. When caring for those at the end of life, they often express the desire to be out of pain and suffering from illness. They are tired of having to take all those medications.

Those who are dying from long-term illnesses have more time to process the idea of dying and are more accepting of the inevitability of death. They seem to have a better sense of peace and acceptance because they have a very good idea about how they are going to die.

In 2020, everyone was faced with the brutal wave of death from the coronavirus disease (COVID 19) pandemic with more than 5, 778, 264 deaths worldwide.

The saddest thing about Covid is many did not get the chance to bury their loved ones.

That funeral service ritual was missing in most countries. Many waited with anxiety trying to find out the fate of their loved ones in the hospital. Many were praying for that 50%

chance of survival. COVID-19 forced the world to accept something we never saw coming.

People were dying alone at hospitals. The norm of families coming to say their final goodbyes was taken away from them, and it was heart-breaking, especially when as a nurse you had to break the news. Relatives would ask if their loved one was alone. Of course, we know the answer. But they just asked for their peace of mind.

If anyone were to ever tell us that for the past two years, we would be at the mercy of the pandemic that has claimed so many lives. We would most likely say no. It has all been like a dream or a scene out of a movie, not the reality of life.

As covid started to release its hold on the world, and we appear to be in a better position to manage it, Russia invaded Ukraine and the war began. Fear of a third world war has become the talk around the world. And thousands of civilians and soldiers have lost their lives.

Death will never go away. As long as we are living, it will happen every second around us.

Chapter Takeaways

1. Let go of the guilt and feelings that you could have done something to prevent your loved one from passing.

2. Forgive yourself. Let go of the judgments you think others have or are holding against you. Stop feeling responsible for the death of a loved one, especially if you are a health care professional.

3. Understand that death and loss are outside of our control.

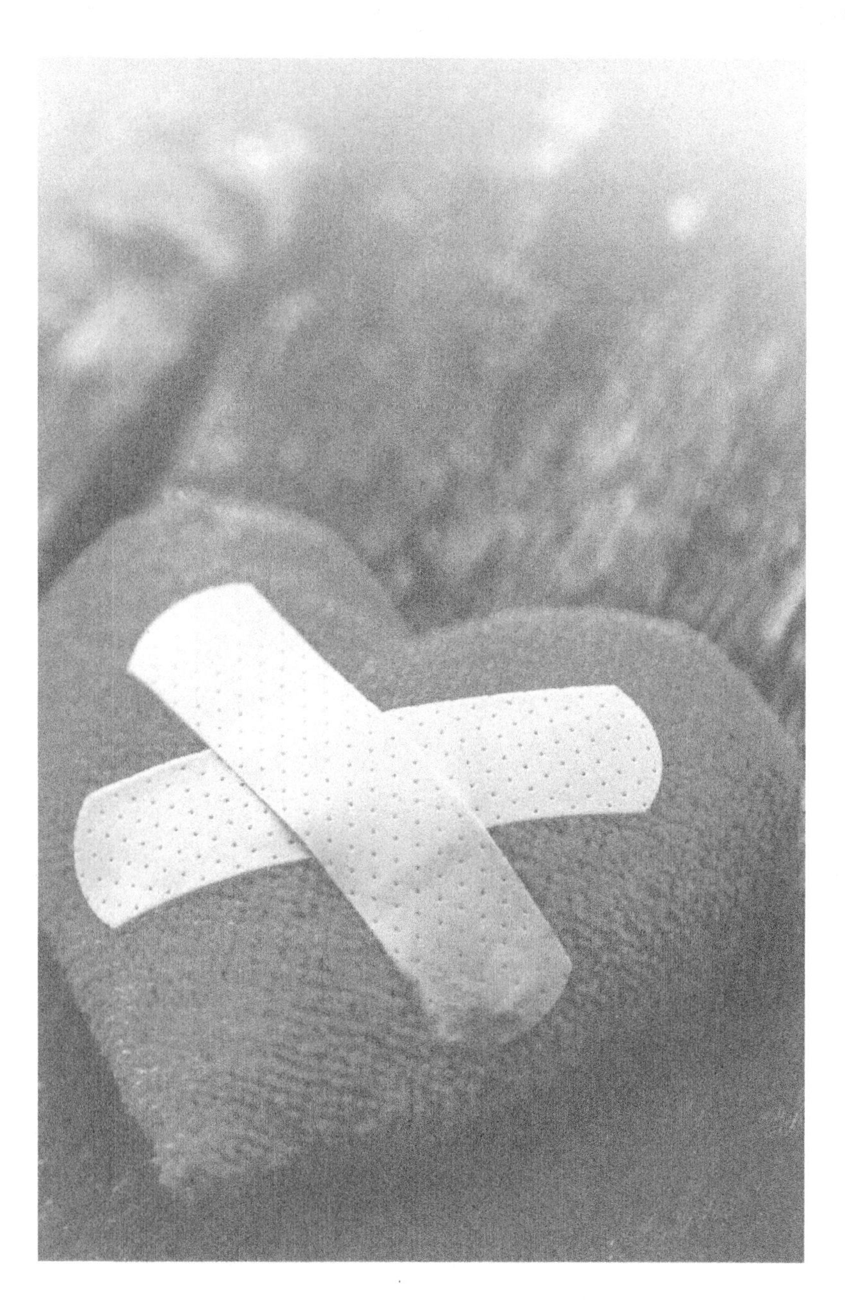

CHAPTER 7

A Grieving Family

"You don't choose your family.
They are God's gift to you, as you are to them."
— **DESMOND TUTU**

To me, family is everything. Those who know me know everything I do is about my family. I celebrate my family, those who support, inspire, and encourage me along the way. My family has played a very important part in my life, including my childhood.

What happens when the glue that keeps the family together is gone? How are you supposed to cope when that person is no more? In our case, it was my mother, and I struggled to imagine life without her. Mom would have known what to do today and just what to say to make me feel better.

She would have known just how to solve our problems and when to step in if my siblings and I had a disagreement.

How did she do it?

She normally woke up at the crack of dawn. By the time we got up, our breakfast would be waiting for us. The smell of her food would greet my hungry belly every morning as I fought to get myself up so I would not be late for school. Talking about my mother's cooking, three days after Mom's burial, my nephew asked me to make them some doughnuts. So, I ventured on Pinterest in search of the perfect recipe.

I thought I did it justice. The doughnut was soft and golden, well-covered with cinnamon sugar. I called them into the kitchen to have their share. However, my nephew was not as happy with the doughnuts as I was. He let me know they didn't have enough sugar like Granny's. It was good but not as good as hers. They would make those remarks every time they asked me to do something for them.

I realized that even at their age, they could tell the recipe I was using wasn't the original. My mother did not follow any kind of instructions when cooking, and she did not own a measuring scale, cups, or spoons but she always got the balance right.

Our lives lost balance when our mother died. It was like living on a seesaw.

She would comb my hair, have our packed lunch ready and still get out of the house on time to get to work. She did everything gracefully and at ease, like a pro, a superwoman with special powers. She was a single mother who made life seem easy.

Now that our mother is gone, my feet are too small to fit into her grand shoes, although, in reality, our shoe sizes are the same. As the firstborn, a lot of the responsibilities lay heavily on my shoulder, and the weight is dislocating it from the socket. Making decisions seems ten times harder. It was easier with Mom around. We would talk it out together, and she would advise what was best.

Unknowingly, I took on the role of the mother, rather than the older sister my siblings knew and loved. I wasn't treating them like the adults they are but instead, I was making decisions for them as if they were still children in need of parental guidance. As with any other family, we would have little disagreements. However, trying to be the problem solver and solution to everything, I failed to realize that my siblings were all living their individual lives.

Merila, a parent of two herself, was making her decisions independently. She is an adult and more than capable of making independent and informed choices. She did not need me to tell her how to live her life.

I only realized this when I started the Speaker Mentor Program where I had to write my story. God started revealing things to me. He started showing me the love I have for my siblings and that they needed me to show up emotionally. They needed my love and bond, a relationship where we can talk about any and everything. We failed to have conversations with each other to express how we feel.

I forgot that they went through the death ordeal twice and both times, they had front row seats. They were there physically when Mom was rushed to the hospital and when Curliana had the seizure, and they could do nothing about it.

While we grieved, we failed to communicate. Someone like me who never passed an opportunity to talk, never engaged my siblings, daughter, nieces, nephew, or grandmother about how they truly felt.

The aftercare advice I would give to my patients' relatives, I did not give to my family. I fell short of simply asking them how they felt, what they were thinking, and if they were okay.

I failed.

I was trying to be there for them, but I was not there in the way they needed me. All the knowledge I had went out through the window at the very time I should have used it. I thought they were coping. I took it for granted they were alright. But just like me, they were hiding their grief.

On the outside, to those looking in, we appear to be doing well but, on the inside, it can be terrifying. We sometimes display behaviors that are out of character. The love that exists is replaced by anger and frustration.

I vividly remember a few days after Mom's burial, my sister and I had a disagreement. It wasn't pleasant. Afterward, I felt a wave of shame.

Within, I was fighting to justify my behavior and tell others what had transpired. It might have just been a moment of madness, but I was certain I heard my mom's voice saying, "I am not pleased with you. You are the oldest and should know better."

At that point, I felt a rush of guilt that I had disappointed my dead mother. I apologized to my sister. However, I still failed to see she too was grieving.

I am not saying what she did was right, but grief time can push us to the edge, and others around us will suffer or even be abused if we are not careful.

In our home, we were selfishly trying to cope with our own grief, but one very clear thing was we never gave up on each other. The fact is each of us was hit by the wave of life at the speed of lightning on the same day and in the same year. We lost a part of ourselves. We lost our mother. We lost our sister.

We lost our uncle, aunties, cousins, friends, and immediate family members.

We all shared the loss and felt the hurt and void. We all spoke the same grief language, "I miss you." We all acknowledged we would never hear our loved one's voices, see, or touch them again. The pain is real.

When my sister and I disagreed, my aunties told us they did not expect that from my mother's children. And I understand why. My mother was the ever-loving, ever caring one.

My challenge is they expressed their disappointment but never found out how we were doing. We were left craving a mother's love, affection, warmth, and words of advice. She always knew what to say, how to pray, and how to bring peace to conflict.

We failed their expectations and did so badly. I did not know we were expected to act differently. We fell way below the bar they set for us. It crumbled to the ground and so did we. Grief can cause the impossible.

Although not in the best of health, we still have our granny. This woman, Justina Sealys, is known to many in the community as Acha. Sometimes, I wonder if she ever grieved her many losses. In a short time, she lost three of her children and one granddaughter whom she raised. When I look at her, it does not show.

After reading and researching, I learned even though people don't show their sadness, it doesn't mean they are not grieving. Granny carries it well with ease and grace. She shows up for everyone. She is never absent; just call, and she will be right there. She is a strong woman, a hustler, and a survivor.

My grandmother has been a diabetic for almost half of her life, and she knows how to take care of her health. Before, she never once had uncontrolled blood sugar levels but in the past month, she has had two episodes of her blood sugar reading being too high. The local wellness center had to send her to the hospital. Her blood pressure had also elevated. She was showing up for everyone, and we failed to notice that her grief was taking a toll on her health.

My granny is a lovely individual. Her love knows no boundaries when it comes to her family. She loved us all with equal measure. She is the first for everything. She is the first at the hospital bed, the first to show up with a bowl full of soup. She would show up with lunch or dinner, even though she knows we are more than capable of cooking our own meals. Most times, we had already eaten, or our food would have just finished cooking when she appeared. Yet, religiously, she did not come over empty-handed.

Granny stayed over at our house for weeks during the passing of my sister and again during the passing of my mom. She did the same with my cousins when my uncle and aunt passed away.

She was that physical strength we needed at the time. She is my very own guardian angel on the earth.

Granny only emotionally expresses her grief with a few screaming matches at the church and graveside. There were days when I observed her with the eyes of a nurse and not as her granddaughter. I saw signs of depression. She would sit in the doorway gazing into the distant sky, lost in thought with her hand under her chin. When you ask her what she is thinking about she would say "nothing." But the image of someone grieving was all I could see.

I am certain our family is not the only one that avoids talking about grief and death, no matter how often we encounter death in the family. But I have learned talking about is important if you want to experience healing and find freedom from the guilt and pain. When you carry those unexpressed feelings day in and day out, it is damaging physically, psychologically, spiritually, and emotionally.

Many online articles say that coping with grief is one of the most difficult challenges you can face, not only in terms of your emotional health. In fact, grief can negatively affect our physical health as well.

Research also highlights some of the most common health problems caused by grief: heart problems, depression, weakened immune system, as well as alcohol and substance abuse.

It is said that broken heart syndrome can occur from the stress of events such as grief, divorce, or death. This happens when the heart fails to pump normally, even in healthy people.

Health experts believe that a rapid increase in stress hormones such as adrenaline can temporarily damage the heart.

Broken heart syndrome may be mistaken for a heart attack as the pain can be so intense in the chest region. This condition is treatable.

My aunty reported a couple of days after my mother's burial that she wasn't feeling well and would go to the health center the next morning for a check-up. Her vitals were taken, and her blood pressure was at a dangerously high level. At that moment, we did not realize it was the effect of the grief she was going through.

On most afternoons, my mother would leave our home to visit my aunt and uncle at their home. In fact, that was where she was coming from when I received the call of her passing. When my mother's siblings came to our house, she always walked with them to where they lived, spending hours talking on the way. She would not return until later. They had a special bond that we did not understand. They would see each other off at a halfway point.

I could never understand their pain, but the silence is unbearable. The bottling up of the pain is showing up in their health and they don't see the damage in it. Through the pain, they showed up for us as we prepared for my mother and sister's funeral.

They were the chefs and the flower arrangers and filled any role necessary. They did all they could to ensure the day went by smoothly. My uncles did all the heavy lifting and the cleaning around the place in preparation for the day. They were the reason everything went well.

One thing about my family is that some of them know how to cry and scream at a funeral. It's that painful scream, which takes all the energy from inside you.

As sad as a funeral is, it is a place where families come together to express their love for the deceased and share loving memories of that person.

After the service is the time you get to learn a little more about the person's childhood and things you didn't know about. You come face to face with strangers they had an impact on during their lifetime.

During the process of writing this book, my family wrote an account of the loss of my mother and sister.

Latisha is my daughter and Mommy's first granddaughter. She raised her while I was away in the army. I was a teen mom, and my mother never left me or gave up on me. She took care of my daughter and me. She was never ashamed to walk the streets with me and her grandchild, even though I may have disappointed her, she never once let it show.

Mommy went against family advice when it came to her granddaughter and me, those who felt I should not be in her care anymore because I was pregnant. I was determined to rise above the criticism from my family and be a better version of myself for the sake of my mother and daughter. I was prepared to prove them wrong.

But not too long after, the same ones who wanted to tell my mother how to run her household were in the same position as her. Their daughter became a teenage mother, even at a younger age than me. Did they send her to live with her child's father?

No, they didn't. But they wanted my mother to.

I was glad my mother never took their advice and she taught me how to raise my daughter. She taught me how to love and care for her. I promised my mother that I would never disappoint her or bring shame to her household again.

My constant prayer was, "Lord, I will never have another baby until I am married or in a position where I am financially stable." I can tell you God kept His promise and I kept mine. My daughter is now 23 years old and an only child.

When I asked Latisha how she feels about the loss of her grandmother and aunty this is what she wrote:

Their halos shine brightly; their legacies live on.
Mommy, I miss you.
Words cannot express the pain I feel.
People say time lessens the pain, but I beg to differ.
When we received the call, I prayed so much. No! Not Mommy!

It can't be! Lord, why? So many questions with no answers.
The hardest part was the distance, the pain in my heart felt like a tumor.
I still remember the day we laid you down.
Your face is frozen in blissful eternal sleep.
A last tearful glance as you were taken away.
There was nothing anyone could do or say.

My pleas and tears didn't bring you back to me.
Comforting friends could not help me to see.
No words could explain my grieving heart.
Why cruel death had to tear our world apart.

Sometimes memories return from photos
or suddenly come to mind in the strangest moments.

I miss our chats and hour-long conversations on the phone.
You would fill me in and make sure I didn't miss a thing.
I miss you singing randomly, even when you didn't know the lyrics and made them up as you sang.

I miss your long spiritual talks to remind me who I am and what I am capable of.
I miss your smile, your laughter, and your silly jokes.
Every moment reminds me that you loved us and truly cared.
I will forever treasure those memories deep in my heart.
Ensuring that you are with me as a part of my heart
to comfort and sustain me until I see you once more.

I hope you said hi to Curliana for us.
Tell her how much we miss her and how much things have changed.
Her babies have grown so much.
You taught me how to be strong and independent.
You taught me how to love
and most importantly, how to pray.
You said in whatever we do, love God unconditionally.

You showed us how to be selfless yet content.
I wish you didn't leave me so soon but I am forever
grateful for the lessons learned and the strong bond we had.
❤ *I love and miss you Maah Grandma Bear* ❤
Rest, my angel until we meet again 🕊 *21.03.20* 🕊

My daughter is not one to express her emotions. She tends to isolate herself. She would rather spend time alone in her room. Although it's hard at times, I have learned to give her space; when she is ready to talk, she will.

Sometimes she spends full days without talking to me, apart from saying good morning and goodnight. She expresses her pain better by writing on her status and doesn't speak it out. I know when she is in a low mood, so when I notice she's having those moments I try to engage her in a conversation; this doesn't always work.

When browsing other family members' social media pages, I could see all the sad and painful posts that seem much easier to write than to verbalize. Every single social media story brings tears to my heart as I read. I could almost express their pain.

Here are some excerpts:

"Our hearts are broken beyond repair. This news that I received this morning is a hard pill to swallow." One of my cousins expressed this on her Facebook page.

"Who am I going to call to come and babysit my girls" stated one of my cousins after my sister died. "You were my best friend and this morning I woke up wanting to call you, but you are not there."

The tributes continue to pour out on everyone's pages, "I light this candle for someone who is no longer here with us."

"We are yet again struck by the brutal hands of death. Lord, we can't take this pain anymore." This was loaded with broken heart emojis and tearful eyes.

Many had stories to tell about their feelings, but they told them in their own subtle and profound ways. It is sad, and we all had to acknowledge we would not see them again, not anytime soon.

My brother expressed his grief so much different from us. My brother is disabled, and his speech is not always clear, but we understand him. Though he is disabled, he is very independent.

During his tender years, we were very protective of him but as he got older and started doing things his own way, we had to learn to let go. He likes building chicken cages and planting his seeds and food. He also does most of the weeding around the house. He considers himself the man of the house and would express his disappointment if we did something he wasn't pleased about. He is very loving and adores his nieces and nephew. I would say he spoils them. He seldom returns home from his outings without bringing them a treat.

I can't recall seeing my brother cry before my sister's death. However, the day I received the news of my sister's passing, I could hear him crying. The deal breaker was on the day of the funeral when no one could support him. He was on all fours on the ground in tears.

He was in pain and very sad. He became very protective of my sister's children, and it was very difficult trying to correct my niece without my brother getting upset. Sometimes I would be talking to my niece, and he would come to get her saying I was shouting at her. He had become sensitive to loud conversations.

He started hiding rum bottles under his pillow in his room. The first time I discovered it was on a day I decided to clean his room; something he did for himself. He seldom left his room untidy but after my sister's death, he would not clean as much as he did.

As a custom in St. Lucia, people would come over to the house from the day the person dies until the burial. Hence, my brother had the rum that he would drink at night with them. He was never a heavy drinker but since our mother's death, my sister has reported on many occasions that he returns to the house drunk.

Mom's death was the final straw I believe. On the day of the burial, he made a wooden cross covered with flowers and took it to the place where my mother was found before being taken to the hospital. We never really talked about it, so I don't know how he feels and what is going on inside his head. I have thought of getting counseling for him and as a family, I hope we can engage in some group therapy.

My baby sister is the last of the bunch. We nicknamed her "Baby" because she was very clingy to my mother, or maybe it was the other way around. She has epilepsy and suffers from quite a few seizures. Everywhere my mother went, you would see my sister. Mom found it very hard to let go when my sister had to travel to the north of the country for school. She eventually did, but not without its share of worries. Most of the calls I received were when my sister had an attack. My mother was her best friend, and they did everything together: going to church, taking walks, etc. They washed together and my mother chose to sleep next to my sister so she would not miss when she was having a seizure.

I only witnessed my sister having a seizure once and within seconds everyone in the house knew what to do. Instantly, she was back to herself again. Mother made sure she had her meals on time and took her medication. She had OCD when it came to my baby sister.

Hence, I was shocked when I received the call that my other sister was the one who had a seizure and died. We were over-protective of my sister. We were concerned that if we left her at home alone, she might have a seizure, and no one would be there to help her. We had an idea of the lives lost due to seizures and that was one of our greatest fears as a family. We did not really talk about it but the was always at the back of our minds.

When my mother passed, my sister became very withdrawn from us. I know she misses our mother. She would often sit alone in silence and refuse to let us in. Before Mom's death, we would have long conversations. Now, it's difficult to get two words out of her when I call.

I am not sure if she is happy or sad. I don't want to take my mother's space in her life, but I would give anything for her to tell me how she feels. She has definitely changed. Even her visits to Grandma are not as frequent.

Grief doesn't only affect you but those close to you. My boy-friend puts up with me, but, at times, I feel undeserving of his love and affection. I am fully aware that I lost my mother, but I need to acknowledge he had a relationship with her too. I have never heard him cry. I saw the tears in his eyes when his dad passed away a few months before my mother. But for her death, his crying was different. He literally wailed. I believe it is because, at the time, his grief over the loss of his dad was still a fresh wound that needed to be healed, so the death of my mom possibly made him revisit that pain.

Our family made some mistakes as we faced multiple deaths. I hope you don't do the same. If your family has lost a loved one, talk about your individual pain. Even though you live in the same household, you can never tell what the other person is experiencing.

You owe it to yourself to find that time and space to open up to each other. Chances are that your feelings and emotions are the same and together you can navigate through them. Don't think your family doesn't care because they do not grieve like you.

You are not the only one dealing with those waves of emotions. Take the lead. Be the one brave enough to say I am not coping.

As a family, we know that we have been through a lot over the past seven years, but we try to find ways to move forward from there. Birthdays and anniversaries of our beloved are hard and at those moments, sometimes, you may feel like being on your own. However, being together helps lessen the pain.

It is hard to notice when children are going through grief. Sometimes the things they do to get your attention are always questionable. I can tell you we haven't gotten it right when it comes to my nieces, Abney and Darnella, and my nephew Jerbarry.

My mother spoiled the three of them, and we would always refer to them as Mommy's handbag, especially Abney.

The only place mother would not be with Abney was at school but everywhere else she would take her along. The lady loved her grandchildren, and the love was reciprocated. My mother's role in Abney's life was that of a grandmother and a mother because she was only three years old when her mother died.

I personally thought she was too young to have even noticed the death of her mother, too young to understand what death was, but I was wrong. I failed her. It was not until my mother's death in 2020 that I realized Abney was grieving. The kids always take my phone when I am around, and one day, before my mother's burial, I was going through my phone when I noticed a video recording by her. She said:

"I miss my mother and my granny. They died and they are in heaven looking down on us. I love my aunties, my uncle, my brother, and my cousin. I don't want them to die because I will be alone if they do. I don't want my grandmother to die because I will be very sad again. Thank you for watching my YouTube channel." The child had a whole imaginary channel while she made her recording.

We often make the mistake of not giving children enough credit and ignoring their feelings. We try to downplay the realities in their lives and cycles are repeated. We don't talk about the events of life and that death will happen when we least expect it.

Breaking that cycle helps healing and growth. It helps to prepare us for the things in life that we can't and will not be able to avoid.

You can have all the knowledge in life, you can be the expert on a subject but when it happens in your family you become the most inexperienced person ever. You must step out of the profession and become a loved one. Feel the pain of others and help them move on.

Abney was grieving differently from us she was craving the love of a mother and grandmother. As she said in her recording, she loved us, and she acknowledged they are no longer around. I was treating her like a baby although she had already passed that stage.

I realize she does not want a replacement for her mother or granny, she just wants to be loved by me the same way they loved her. She wants to know and be reassured that we will always be there for her. As time went on, we noticed a change in Abney's behavior, and we tried to solve the problem without dealing with its roots. She was losing interest in school and homework and would engage in every other activity than her schoolwork. We tried everything possible from Zoom to WhatsApp video calls. Nothing worked. She did not want to do things she used to love. She would pretend she was asleep when it was prayer time, which was unusual. She loved to pray with my mother when she was alive. Her behavior was becoming challenging, and we thought she was seeking attention.

After I started the Speaker Mentorship Program, it dawned on me that Abney needed counseling. Actually, Rafati had already mentioned it to me. So, after one of my sessions, I reached out to a counselor he recommended. We set up a Zoom meeting and I told her about my niece's behavior. We agreed on a referral and now, my niece is going to counseling. It is better to deal with a child's mental health now, instead of trying to repair a broken adult later in life.

After my mother's burial, when school reopened in September 2020, I went to the school to speak to Abney's principal. I was referring her for therapy, but I was not successful.

The principal herself was grieving as she had lost her husband suddenly a year prior. She told me that if I had come to see her a year earlier to talk about my loss and the help I was seeking for my niece, she would not have seen me.

She said she was not ready to talk to anyone about death during that time of her life. The subject was just hateful and too painful to talk about. She said though she sympathizes with others, she wasn't prepared to partake and that was a no-go zone at the time. I understood how she felt.

We spoke at length about our emotions and the feeling of losing someone so close to you suddenly. We conversed about the ways you must learn to adjust without the person, especially if that person took care of everything. Having to navigate life without the chain that kept the family together takes a lot out of you.

We spoke about how a day wouldn't go by without being heavy with tears and hiding for hours away from others so they don't see the tears in our eyes and that we are unable to cope. As we conversed, we realized we had the same feelings about our loss. But the most important thing is having people around you who understand your state of mind at the time without the need for words.

Before the end of our meeting, she told me she needed to talk and let it out. The feeling of being heard and understood was liberating.

"You did not come to my office by chance; this was appointed," she said.

"Thank you so much for being open with me. I have only gone through it once, but you did twice, and your strength is amazing."

God knew I needed that interaction and He set the meeting up for us. Our meeting ended with tears in our eyes and a hug. I also told her about the impact her husband had on my life growing up. He was the choirmaster.

Sometimes we meet people who remind us it is okay to not be okay as you are not in this alone. There is a community of love around you, especially those who don't judge you. Open your heart to feel others' hearts beating as they are experiencing the same emotions as you.

Her husband's death took me by surprise. He was one of my teachers from primary school. As Jacqueline and I would say, he was our favorite. The role he played in our lives will never go unnoticed. He encouraged us to be the best we can be. He shortened my name to Jermz, and no matter where I was in a crowd, he would call that name. Instantly, I knew it was sir.

My sister Merlia had big shoes to fill. She is now the one at home with the family and the kids. The loss of my mother and sister has forced her to become a mother of four, two of her own and my nieces Abney and Amerila.

As she keeps the home together, I must continue my financial obligation to the family. Between the two of us, we keep the family together. Life had to go on without my mother and my sister and that was the best way we knew how. Her needs and personal growth have been put at a standstill for us to keep moving as a family unit.

I admire my sister's strength and although we don't always see eye to eye, we are learning and growing. In every family, there are disagreements but that doesn't mean we love each other less. Our bond as sisters has always been strong and it has grown as we learn to move forward without the head of our family, the queen of our hearts and fixer of all things.

Just like me, my sister put her pain aside to be there for the family. She is the core in my absence. She is trying to be strong and refuses to let the children see the tears and sadness in her eyes. She is moving with the waves and clouds that overshadow her. She is pushing forward with pain.

She did not only witness one loss but two. Each time, she was there.

The second time she had to leave the kids and run to the place our mother was.

She escorted her to the hospital. She was the first to receive the news, "I am sorry, but your mother has died."

I can't imagine what the weight of that message must have felt like, how she fought back the tears to muster the strength to call me and relay the message. I was broken when I received the news second-hand. I just can't get the image of what her face looked like knowing she was the last person to see Mommy, the one to see her take her last breath, the last to feel her warm breath upon her neck. It pains me just typing those words. As I write this, I feel the urge to call my sister to tell her I know how she feels, and it is okay not to be okay. I want her to know I am here for her, to take her time and breathe through it. We will make it to the other side together.

Our family strives because we communicate and try to meet each other's needs. The changes we made in our own personal growth make us stronger. It strengthens the bond that was already there.

When we miss our mother, we talk and smile at the things she would have done or said. We continue to be vulnerable with each other as we build stronger memories together. Because we lost our mother and sister suddenly, we don't want it to happen again and we regret not living as she wanted us to.

Mom wanted us to be close and that's something I keep at the back of my mind whenever I think of those of us who are still alive. Sometimes it may feel as if we are alone in this, but I have also learned to give them their breathing space to feel their emotions. I can't take it away from them. That's something they must do on their own. They must learn to find ways to cope and navigate through.

You can be living in the same household but experience different emotions. The things you miss about those who died are different. The way you viewed the person is different. Everything is different.

Talk about the things you miss. Talk about your feelings and be willing to give everyone as much time and space necessary to move forward. Beauty is all around when love is in the home. Take the first step to be open. Listen to others' feelings and opinions without judgment. Listen and encourage them to feel the hurt and pain. Don't mask it. Allow it to flow and you will feel better.

My greatest desire for my family and yours is to find release from the journey with grief. The grief we endure can take a toll on our families in many ways, especially when we do not take the time to talk about how we feel openly and allow ourselves to grieve properly. Children are also affected. They may exhibit unusual negative behaviors that must not be ignored. Hence, as I said earlier, we must pay particular attention to how we grieve because the children follow our examples. If we hold it in, they will too, and grief suppression is harmful.

If you have lost a mother or sibling to death, you have experienced a highly stressful life event. But not only you, all of your siblings as well. They too must heal. Otherwise, it can cause mental health, social, and other issues. In many instances, relationships that were once good can turn sour as one person avoids talking and thinking about their deceased loved ones or any reminders of the person. Death can complicate emotions. As I have said in this book, the grieving process is not written in stone. There is no one-size-fits-all because we all grieve differently. However, the process is important and it can help you and your family in your battle with grief:

The Grieving Process

Denial

The first stage in this theory, denial helps us minimize the overwhelming pain of loss. As we process the reality of our loss, we are also trying to survive emotional pain. It can be hard to believe we have lost an important person in our lives, especially when we may have just spoken with this person the previous week or even the previous day.

Our reality has shifted completely in this moment of loss. It can take our minds some time to adjust to this new reality. We are reflecting on the experiences we have shared with the person we lost, and we might find ourselves wondering how to move forward in life without this person.

This is a lot of information to explore and a lot of painful imagery to process. Denial attempts to slow this process down and take us through it one step at a time, rather than risk the potential of feeling overwhelmed by our emotions.

Denial is not only an attempt to pretend that the loss does not exist. We are also trying to absorb and understand what is happening.

Anger

It is common to experience anger after the loss of a loved one. We are trying to adjust to a new reality, and we are likely experiencing extreme emotional discomfort. There is so much to process that anger may feel like it allows us an emotional outlet.

Keep in mind that anger does not require us to be very vulnerable. However, it tends to be more socially acceptable than admitting we are scared. Anger allows us to express emotion with less fear of judgment or rejection.

Unfortunately, anger tends to be the first thing we feel when we start to release emotions related to loss. This can leave you feeling isolated in your experience and perceived as unapproachable by others in moments when we could benefit from comfort, connection, and reassurance.

Bargaining

When coping with loss, it isn't unusual to feel so desperate that you are willing to do almost anything to alleviate or minimize the pain. Losing a loved one can cause us to consider any way we can avoid the current pain or the pain we are anticipating from loss. There are many ways we may try to bargain.

Bargaining can come in a variety of promises including:

"God, if you can heal this person I will turn my life around."

"I promise to be better if you will let this person live."

"I'll never get angry again if you can stop him/her from dying or leaving me."

When bargaining starts to take place, we are often directing our requests to a higher power, or something bigger than we are that may be able to influence a different outcome. There is an acute awareness of our humanness in these moments when we realize there is nothing we can do to influence change or a better end result.

This feeling of helplessness can cause us to react in protest by bargaining, which gives us a perceived sense of control over something that feels so out of control. While bargaining we also tend to focus on our personal faults or regrets. We might look back at our interactions with the person we are losing and note all of the times we felt disconnected or may have caused them pain.

It is common to recall times when we may have said things we did not mean, and wish we could go back and behave differently. We also tend to make the drastic assumption that if things had played out differently, we would not be in such an emotionally painful place in our lives.

Depression

During our experience of processing grief, there comes a time when our imaginations calm down and we slowly start to look at the reality of our present situation. Bargaining no longer feels like an option and we are faced with what is happening.

We start to feel the loss of our loved one more abundantly. As our panic begins to subside, the emotional fog begins to clear and the loss feels more present and unavoidable.

In those moments, we tend to pull inward as the sadness grows. We might find ourselves retreating, being less sociable, and reaching out less to others about what we are going through.

Although this is a very natural stage of grief, dealing with depression after the loss of a loved one can be extremely isolating.

When we come to a place of acceptance, it is not that we no longer feel the pain of loss. However, we are no longer resisting the reality of our situation, and we are not struggling to make it something different.

Sadness and regret can still be present in this phase, but the emotional survival tactics of denial, bargaining, and anger are less likely to be present.

Acceptance

When we come to a place of acceptance, it is not that we no longer feel the pain of loss. However, we are no longer resisting the reality of our situation, and we are not struggling to make it something different.

Sadness and regret can still be present in this phase, but the emotional survival tactics of denial, bargaining, and anger are less likely to be present. (Jodi Clarke, MA. "What to Know about the Five Stages of Grief." Verywell Mind. Verywell Mind, February 12, 2021. https://www.verywellmind.com/five-stages-of-grief-4175361).

Chapter Takeaways

1. Be a good listener, especially when children are involved. Be patient and honest with them about your own feelings and show affection. Let them know grief is a part of life. In some instances, avoid questioning them as their answers are very simple.

2. Allow yourself to be vulnerable around your family members. Let them see you cry as it will send a positive message that even the brave cry and crying is not associated with weakness.

3. Share the responsibility with your family as you let go of being overly protective. Don't judge them or be quick to correct them. Always seek professional help and remember that even though you are from the same household, everyone is at a different stage in the grieving process.

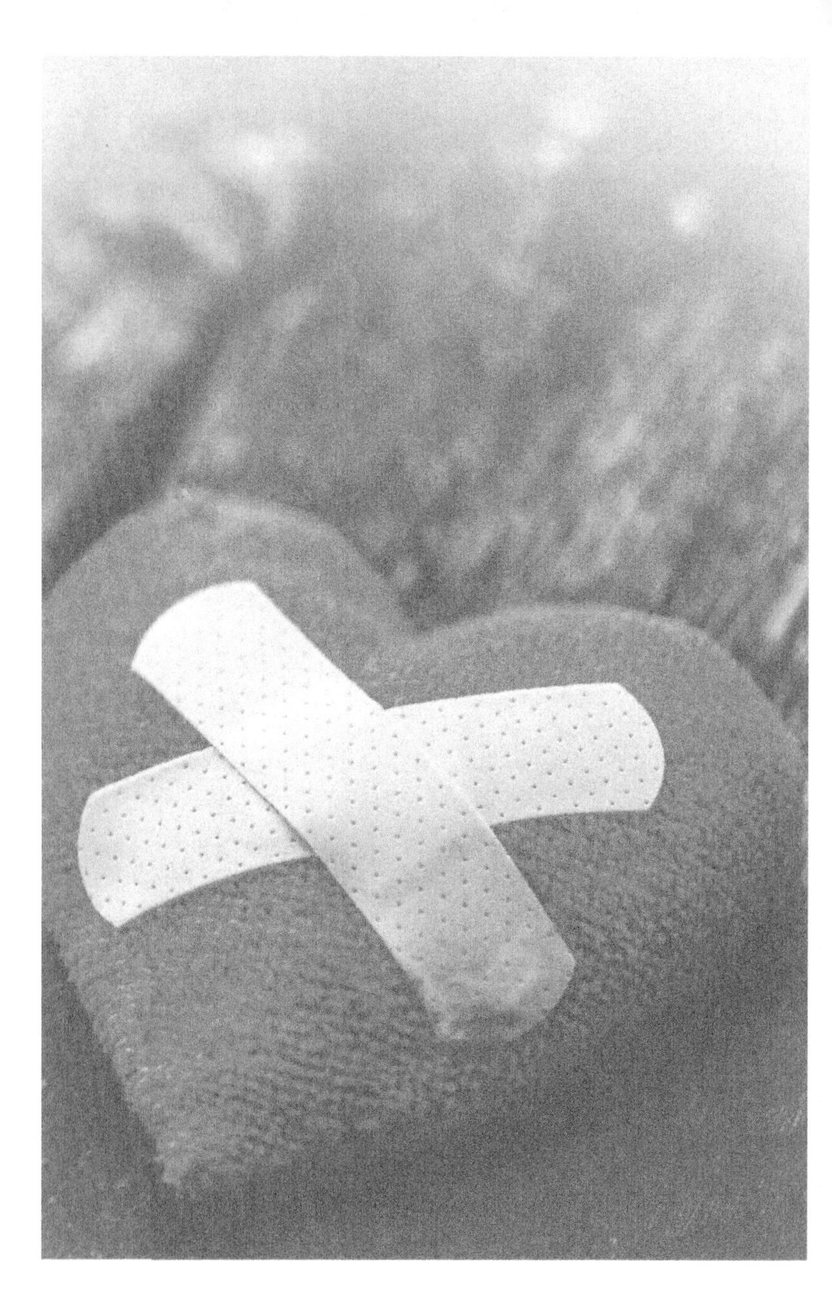

CHAPTER 8

Does It Ever Heal?

"Healing takes courage, and we all have courage, even if we have to dig a little to find it."
—TORI AMOS

People often say during interviews when sharing their stories of the traumatic experiences in their lives: "I don't look like what I have been through."

Can you imagine the opposite of that statement? You would be able to see all the fear and pain the person standing next to you is going through. What would be your reaction toward that person? Chances are that you encounter many hurting people daily. They may be standing in the supermarket line in front of you, sitting next to you in the bus or train station, waiting in the toilet queue, at your workplace, in a doctor's office, or even in your home.

The truth is it is very difficult to tell what individuals around us are going through. We don't know the pressure they face every day. Many people may be dealing with a period of grief. The person next to you might have lost a loved one, a job, a friendship, a pet, and the list goes on. Everyone is hurting and we will never know what each person we meet is going through. Grief is unique and no two people experience it the same or go through the grieving process in the actual order.

I have learned too well that there isn't a step-by-step order in which to grieve. The five stages of the grief cycle are denial, anger, bargaining, depression, and acceptance (Elisabeth Kubler-Ross). But they don't follow a specific order, and, in some instances, individuals may not even experience any of the five stages.

These five stages of grief were proposed in 1969, inspired by Kuber-Ross' work with terminally ill patients.

In other cases, only one or three stages might be experienced during your period of grief. The mistake made by many is to believe that once you get to the acceptance stage of grief, your grieving should come to an end, but this is far from reality.

At times, I am forced to revisit my emotions such as anger and sadness, particularly on my loved one's birthdays and the days they died.

I experienced immense guilt on my 40th birthday although I celebrated it with a party with family and friends. I was stuck in a place hoping and wishing my mother and sister were there to see me turn my milestone of 40 years on the earth.

Guilt consumed me as I could not bear the thought that they were not there to tell me how proud they were of me and the person I have grown into. Some days, I just have to allow myself to move with the waves of grief as I try to understand its power and purpose in my life. The days I stop hiding and accept the pain that comes with each wave I feel much better and lighter. I feel able and willing to face tomorrow with a smile.

Grief is like a fingerprint, unique to everyone. You can be from the same household or family, and everyone will experience something different at the same time.

Grief can't be rushed and doesn't have an expiration date. So don't get worried when people tell you that you should have gotten over it by now.

Allow yourself to go through the grieving process. Nothing is wrong with you if you are grieving the loss of a loved one who died decades ago. It is important to allow yourself to feel the emotions we are faced with daily. No two days are the same.

Never run from your emotions and pain just ride with them. It will get better but not instantly. Somedays might hurt more than others but face your pain and acknowledge it.

Stop hiding from grief; show up with it.

Allow yourself to breathe through the pain. That knee you feel crushing your windpipe will eventually start shifting. Learn to find your breathing space through your grief because the loss will always be a part of you. That empty space will always be there. That's the reality.

Someone I considered to be my best friend suddenly got cold with me for no apparent reason. Although I lost that friendship in 2014, the thought of our friendship and the pain of the loss pop up now and then. The things we used to do together and the places we visit bring back memories that are still part of my life story.

Those moments of blame come off and on. I keep searching myself trying to figure out why the friendship ended and if I could have done anything to prevent the breakup.

Moments like these make it hard to move on. You fail to forge other good friendships based on those past painful experiences and, as a result, you miss out on a good and better friendship of love.

During that period of my life, I had serious trust issues and anyone who was seeking to build friendships with me was blocked by a wall of protection I immediately put up.

You see, only those who know us and the break-up of our friendship know the truth.

To other people, I say we just went our separate ways.

I did not realize I was holding on to so much grief, hurt, and pain, and, as a result, I was not moving forward. I was just stuck in a rut trying to figure out what and how things went wrong for the individual to close the door on the friendship.

I did not open myself to healing because I remained stuck in the past. I neglected the love that was around because I was too focused on that one friendship that wasn't there anymore.

As I slowly found myself and started moving forward, I found my healing space as I talked about that friendship. Talking set me free, and I could feel my heart breaking from that long pause it was on for years.

I started writing my feelings down in the form of poems. Beautiful poems that I would share in church during a welcome or Sabbath school program.

I felt free and unchained from the broken friendship as I allowed myself to be loved by others in new friendships. I was assigned to work alongside those two beautiful souls in the Sabbath school department at my church. There, a new rose started blooming again, and I saw life differently. However, now and then, I revisit the pain when I go to places or do things we did together.

If you have made mistakes and you are mad at yourself it's okay. It shows you are human, and you can still feel past the numbness.

Never compare your journey with someone else's. You may have to juggle a group of emotions as you try to balance what's expected of you as "a person in mourning" and your desire for healing.

Grief and loss can be a big moment and a tiny moment at the same time. This is a game-changer in your life. Things will never be the same again after a loss, and that's cool because, otherwise, nothing would be learned.

Shortly after my sister's funeral, I wrote this post on my Facebook page.

Does it heal with time or do we just learn to cope?
They say that time heals but this is a very slow process.
When I look around, I feel the void.
The empty space in my heart.
You will always complete our circle
For your spot, my heart is a label.
I miss you so much today that my heart feels heavy and sore.
As I sit alone I weep. I cry, and I pray.
I wish you could come and talk to me.
I miss you so badly. Rest in peace, my sister. Rest, my love.
It pains my heart for you are no longer here with us.

Facebook became my journal space and every now and then it reminds me of what I was feeling at that time. I had my way with words and grief gave me that. I felt a great sense of calmness after I posted a feed on my timeline.

Writing and talking to those you trust will help you to face your grief head-on and move through its phases more easily. During these phases, it can be very difficult to feel the loving community around us. Don't suffer in silence, allow others to share your feelings and thoughts.

A year after my mother died, I enrolled in the Speaker Mentor Speak Program with my coach. I did not know what to expect, but I knew I wanted to share my grief journey with others. So I signed up, not with any hope of healing from my pain. But telling my story had so much power, I found myself emerging from under the pain that had me buried. A powerful and life-changing experience started taking place.

I shifted gears from being invisible to being seen. I could see my pain and feel it each time it released me.

Oh, how therapeutic it is to write. Every word I typed bubbled the pain to the surface. I couldn't hide it if I tried. There is something so magical about writing that speaking cannot express. As the words flowed from my brain onto the screen before me, I felt them because it was my pain visualized. Untrapped. Unhidden. Free. Released. Unstoppable.

As my mentor encouraged me to write, the memories spilled onto the screen. I never knew I had so many inside. I learned ages ago that our minds are memory banks that only need to be triggered to be unlocked. So I triggered my box of memories to release my unlocked pain. It is then I saw how much pain and unspoken emotions I had carried for the past five years. It all showed up during our group sessions. I was finally able to set my emotions free.

Writing gave me that newfound strength to face my pain, fears, and guilt. I was no longer afraid to feel and let the tears roll freely without shame. Initially, I had carried so much guilt and blame. However, I found that I was no longer chained to them and the feeling I was less of a Christian because I questioned God about the sudden death experience and the loss of close family members.

I did not realize I was drifting from my faith as I was constantly wearing an invisible mask of courage and strength when I felt broken and lost on the inside.

As I acknowledged my emotions, the "wall of fear" finally fell. Instantly, that moment felt so beautiful that finding the right words to express it was virtually impossible.

The weight I was carrying left my shoulders. I set down the bag of stones I was carrying for miles. It is okay to not be okay. I was hiding too long behind "I am okay" when asked how I was doing.

We all do it. Let's face it. It is much easier to say I am fine than to pour out our hearts to someone who does not have the time to listen. We live in a busy society, and everyone is pressed for time.

I needed to show up for myself and then I could be there for others. From the program, I discovered that my family too needed help to heal and not my over-protectiveness.

I learned to let go and say no instead of the easy yes to everything. I needed to let others play their active part in life. I had to release my hold on the family and allow them to find their breathing space as I did.

It has allowed me to share what my family is going through with others facing the same situation in hopes that they know their feelings—whether poured out or hiding on the inside—are okay.

I am now able to see myself past the stages of darkness and when it comes, a golden ray of light envelopes it.

The negative thoughts I believed about why my loved ones died have been replaced by positive thoughts. I have accepted that death is a natural part of life. My faith gives me the hope that I will see my loved ones again.

Does it ever heal? The answer may vary from individual to individual, but one thing I know is we release the pain as we allow the grieving process to take place and move forward with life.

We learn to balance the weight of grief until we get to the point where we are comfortable laying it down.

Chapter Takeaways

1. Fill your life with memories of your loved ones.
2. Take the time to be true to yourself and just talk. It's okay to speak about your loved ones who died; they were a part of your life and will never leave you. They will always be a part of your life journey and story.
3. Seek professional help if you feel you need it.
4. You are never too strong to be weak. That weakness gives you the strength that you never envisioned was there.
5. Support your family as you heal. Time doesn't heal; it just helps you to grow around the pain. It helps you to release and move forward.
6. Never compare your grief with anyone else; no two people grieve the same way. Also, don't listen to anyone who says you should not grieve too long and so hard. Your grief journey is different and unique to you. There is no set timetable for healing, so, therefore, be patient with yourself and let the healing process takes its natural course in your life.
7. Choose to let go of the hurt and pain. Do things that make you happy: going out with friends and family for a meal, watching your favorite movies, going shopping, etc.

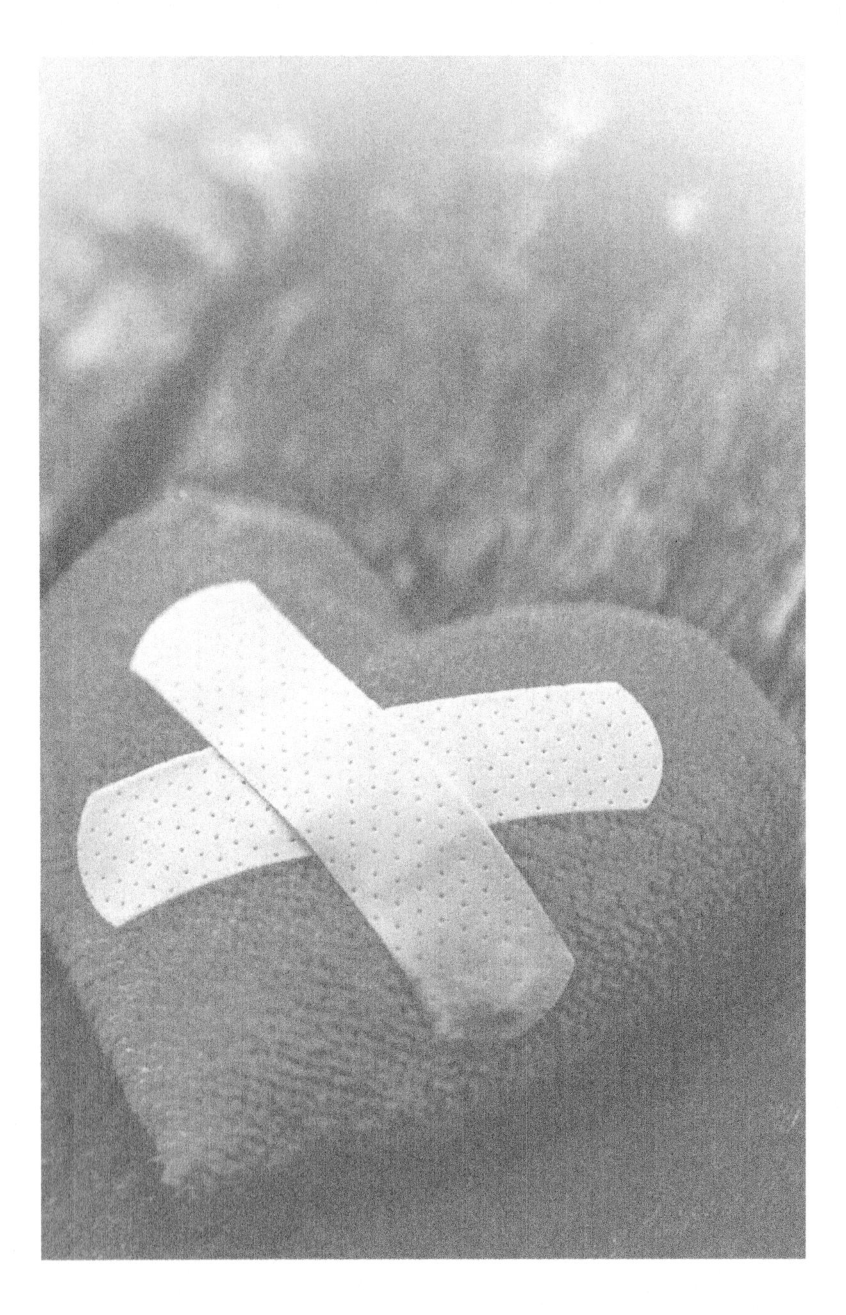

CHAPTER 9

Broken for a Purpose

"If through a broken heart God can bring His purposes to pass in the world, then thank Him for breaking your heart."
—OSWALD CHAMBERS

As I awoke from my labor of pain, sorrows, bitterness, and brokenness, I realized all choices were gone because I had been chained to my fears, struggles, hopelessness, imperfection, guilt, doubts, unworthiness, and an empty spirit.

I had two choices: to allow those chains to hold me down or to break them.

Shuttles have fallen.

Chains have been broken.

My spirit has been set free because my silence has been broken.

My tongue untied as I broke the glass of heaven's floor.

"Talk to Me," He said. "Just talk to Me"

"All I have are questions, Lord."

"Why must an heir to Your kingdom bear such painful experiences to learn certain spiritual truths? Why do I have to taste such bitterness, sorrow, pain, guilt, and fear to understand You?"

He answered, "My daughter, My child, the answer is not always black and white. The answers you are seeking are not always there in plain sight. Just like Hannah, I needed to break the silence, so you can cry Me a river. Just like Jabez, forget your pain because I will bless you and expand your territory. Just like David, you can face your giant because I am here to give you victory."

"But Lord," I whispered, "many times, in my pain and brokenness I forget who You said I am. I forget I am fearfully and wonderfully made. Sometimes I do not feel like an heir to royalty. The pain turns my outer layer into rugs. How can you consider that as royalty or being an heir to Your throne?"

Oh, you see, I was finding excuses to remain chained to my painful bitterness, finding ways to remain hostage to the cage of fear and shame that surrounded me. I was searching for reasons to keep traveling down the tunnel of darkness, rather than finding the crack of light. I was paralyzed with grief and guilt, refusing to walk even if I tried.

I kept throwing pity parties for the cage bird that refused to fly even though it was longing to be set free.

He said, "Take a minute; allow My grace to break those chains.

Allow Me to cut through those barriers and break down those walls."

With teary eyes and a sobbing heart, I answered:

Yes, You can. Yes, I need You to break them down. Take control and take charge. Despite my scars and rugged edges, I am of Your royal priesthood and chosen generation. Just like Shadrach, Meshach, and Abednego, You walk with me through life's fire. When the footsteps fade away and I am too weak, I know You are carrying me. When I feel broken and unworthy, allow me to stare into the skies and get lost in the twilight of the night. But yet, I can't put my finger on it, the awesomeness and wonder of creation.

I go crazy about it but, in my mind, I know there must be a master artist behind it all. He creates something so beautiful it takes all the worries away and brings sweet calmness to troubled souls.

You took my nothingness and created something full of purpose. You never saw the mess but the beauty of brokenness. Under the mask I wear, You expose me layer by layer to show me how much I mean to You. No amount of pain, scars, bitterness, or hurt can lessen Your love for me. Your love is for all eternity. When my back is against the wall, and I am exposed naked to my scars, I feel like royalty with a story to tell the world. It is meant to heal and set free.

When I show up for battle with fear and confront it head-on, I understand I am being equipped to carry on work. So I allow my walls to fall and speak to the Father, asking Him to carry His baby girl.

As I face the ugly truth about myself, I become empowered and driven to help others move past that stage in their lives by acknowledging the pain.

When I face my giant head-on, I remember my mother's favorite Scripture text, "For God has not given you a spirit of fear but of power and of love and of a sound mind" (2 Timothy 1:7).

When I am at my lowest, I remember I can do all things through Christ who strengthens me (Philippians 4:13).

Though I was broken beyond repair, God put my pieces back together again. He will do the same for you. It may take seconds, minutes, hours, days, weeks, months, or years but He is ready to put your pieces back together again.

He took me through the journey to show me my purpose and to birth it through the help of a God-fearing mentor set apart to guide me along the journey.

God will turn your pain to purpose. He did it for me and that's how this book came to life. The career path I chose wasn't by chance; it was divinely appointed—from soldier to nurse. Both equipped me with strong morals and values I needed to be strong and resilient. I now understand that before I was created, God had a plan for my life and with every step I took, He was instructing it.

"For I know the plans I have for you
declares the Lord,plans to prosper you and not to harm you,
plans to give you hope and a future"
(JEREMIAH 29:11).

God loves us, and it is never His intention to see us broken and damaged. When we hurt, He hurts too.

As I reflected on my faith while going through my trials in life, I was reassured it is okay to question God. I blamed Him because it was the easiest thing to do at the time.

During those darkest moments, I could not see or feel His loving arms wrapped around me. I felt alone and betrayed by God. I thought He was being unfair. I had no idea what He wanted from me or what I needed to do. However, it is often said there is always a lesson in the experience you are going through.

If you are grieving, you are going through it for a purpose. You may not understand it now. Although others try to encourage you, they have no idea what the reason is. It took me a while to understand the purpose and the assignment behind my grieving heart, but I found it.

My mentor calls this pregnant with purpose. I discovered that I was already at the pre-labor stage when I booked that discovery call. This pregnancy of purpose was already planned, and every step was in place. I just had to show up.

You see, pregnancy was overdue. I had been carrying it for years, rather than nine months. Take a walk back with me to my very own pregnancy. Although I wasn't ready for motherhood, I had to carry my daughter for nine months.

I saw the disappointment in the eyes of those who did not approve. I felt the shame I caused my mother who was looking forward to me going to my first job after my exam results were out.

Instead of working, I was battling morning sickness, pain, sleepless nights, and adjusting to the changes in my body. When I saw my priceless daughter on the day of delivery, all the pain, guilt, and shame faded away as if they were never there.

Now, I understand this purpose is created out of painful and dark moments. As you embrace those moments you can become better. With God's strength, you can turn your pain into power.

I know that as I share my story, I have become free and powerful, and I am healing. I was challenged by my mentor to achieve my dream no matter how painful the story is. The more you tell it, the more you become empowered.

My mentor constantly reminded us to do it unashamed and fearless. It took me a while to figure out why my mother loved Timothy 1:7, "For God has not given you a spirit of fear but of power and of love and of a sound mind." I understand that fear is not of God, and it should not be in us. We must do it unafraid and bold. I was using fear to build a wall to keep me imprisoned by my brokenness. That wall I was building encouraged me to stay hidden, taking the power to breathe away from me.

To soar to my full potential, I took one bold step to free me from myself and find help in someone who saw my purpose under those scars before I did.

I stopped questioning God about why me and instead asked, "Why not me?" Who better could tell my story other than me? How would I ever find the courage to tackle a topic that is as taboo as death? How would I find the courage to walk with grief instead of falling victim to its mercy? I faced our battle head-on, bitter and sweet but with no regrets.

I had to succumb to my pain to move forward with my healing and find my reasons for the journey. I had to learn to close it chapter by chapter, page by page.

I had to forgive myself for things I held on to that were causing my pain. All the thoughts I was housing inside, I had to let them go. I had to forgive the people who made the comments in my head. You see, I was harboring lots of negativity toward the comments and the people who made them. They were and are not aware that their words had such effects on me.

I did not have the courage to tell them. I just absorbed it like everything else, hoping it would go away. It never did; instead, it started manifesting itself in my heart causing pain and hurt. With the hurt came a barrier I had put up to defend myself against such interactions.

Pain, hurt, fear, and guilt had to be lifted for purpose to come alive. I had to start saying no to others and yes to me. I had to purposefully position myself with strangers and tell my story. Those ladies are no longer strangers; we are now sisters with a common denominator: telling our stories that held us hostage to our past. We became accountable to each other, and we are discovering the purpose beneath our brokenness no matter what.

We began a journey together that allowed us to be vulnerable with each other, telling and sharing as we help each other rise to our purpose and goals and remind ourselves there is beauty where the pain lies. We show up for ourselves and each other.

One of our sisters continuously reminds us that our cabbages are someone else's compost. Someone needs to be healed from our experiences. Someone needs to be reached from our stories. Our purpose is to reach one broken person, someone out there who believes she is alone in her journey.

With every great journey, your time is right on time. Every diversion will lead you right back to where you were meant to be. Who would have ever imagined this girl would rise after all the pain and darkness she was carrying? Who would have thought she would show up and breathe in the quest of helping others breathe?

I am rising to help you move forward from that point where you got stuck and refuse to move forward. Taking my time while removing that knee from my neck, I found the courage to end that unwanted relationship with grief and loss. I understood that broken crayons still color and can still create the most beautiful drawings you have ever seen.

I found my unstuck moment, the moment to set myself free from those jabbing emotions. I set myself free almost to the point I could feel the weight dropping brick by brick, stone by stone, and layer by layer.

I needed this moment of freedom to breathe, to save myself from drowning, to resurface and be me, to find that inner girl who knows no worry, that inner person who knew what it felt like to feel the breeze on her skin as she crossed the finish line a victor.

I am a winner. I know what it feels like to win a race out of pure stamina. I know what it feels like to run against the wind as your only competition at every bend. I know what it feels like to know at the point the only one standing between the gold medal and you is yourself. A runner focuses only on the tracks ahead; everything else is secondary as you plan every next move to get to the end.

I had to find my way back to my faith that was sliding away at the end of my fingertips. I needed a lifeline to save me. I needed that ah-ha moment. The power supply that was cut off, I needed to find it again. I had to get the power back on as quickly as it went off. And wow, when it returned it ignited the flames that were extinguished by grief and guilt. I started showing up.

I started thinking and moving differently. I could breathe again without much effort.

There is power in your brokenness. But you must accept help and acknowledge your pain.

During my spiritual drought over the past years, I wrestled with whether to pray or read the Bible. One day, out of the blue, the pastor called and asked me to do Bible study with a young lady. I had no idea what to say. There was a greater plan that I would start studying with her on Thursday night via Zoom.

I forced myself to study the night before, and did she show up for our first meeting? You guessed it; she didn't, but that was the only meeting she missed. Although I wasn't giving it 100 percent, she informed me that she liked studying with me and I made it relatable.

From that point, I gave the study time the best of my broken state. I was also doing my speaker mentorship program with the complimentary prayer course. As I started releasing from my pain, I felt empowered to do more to keep writing my story.

I desire to work with others going through the same experiences as me. Hence, this book is written to help you find peace in loss and grief, to help you learn to breathe out the burden and pain, and let you know you are not going through your situation alone. It is time to show up for yourself.

Show up for you. Find the switch in the darkness and turn the light on. Emerge from the waves and learn to float. Find yourself again and move forward with your purpose and goals in mind.

It is time to find the light at the end of the tunnel. Grief will never go away; it is part of our lives. However, you can grow around it. As you normalize and accept your grief and talk about it, you will find peace and healing.

Being broken is not the end of you. Be visible and honest about your journey and you will find the strength to grow and live out your purpose. There is great power in spoken words that help to break the glass wall of silence into a thousand pieces.

Chapter Takeaways

1. Share your grief journey with others. Be open and honest about how you made it through your darkest moments.

2. Writing helps you to release your pain as you put your emotions onto paper.

3. Embrace your faith and beliefs to help you navigate those difficult times while grieving. At first, you may question your faith; however, it is essential to connect with that aspect of your life and gain solace from those principles that keep you in shape.

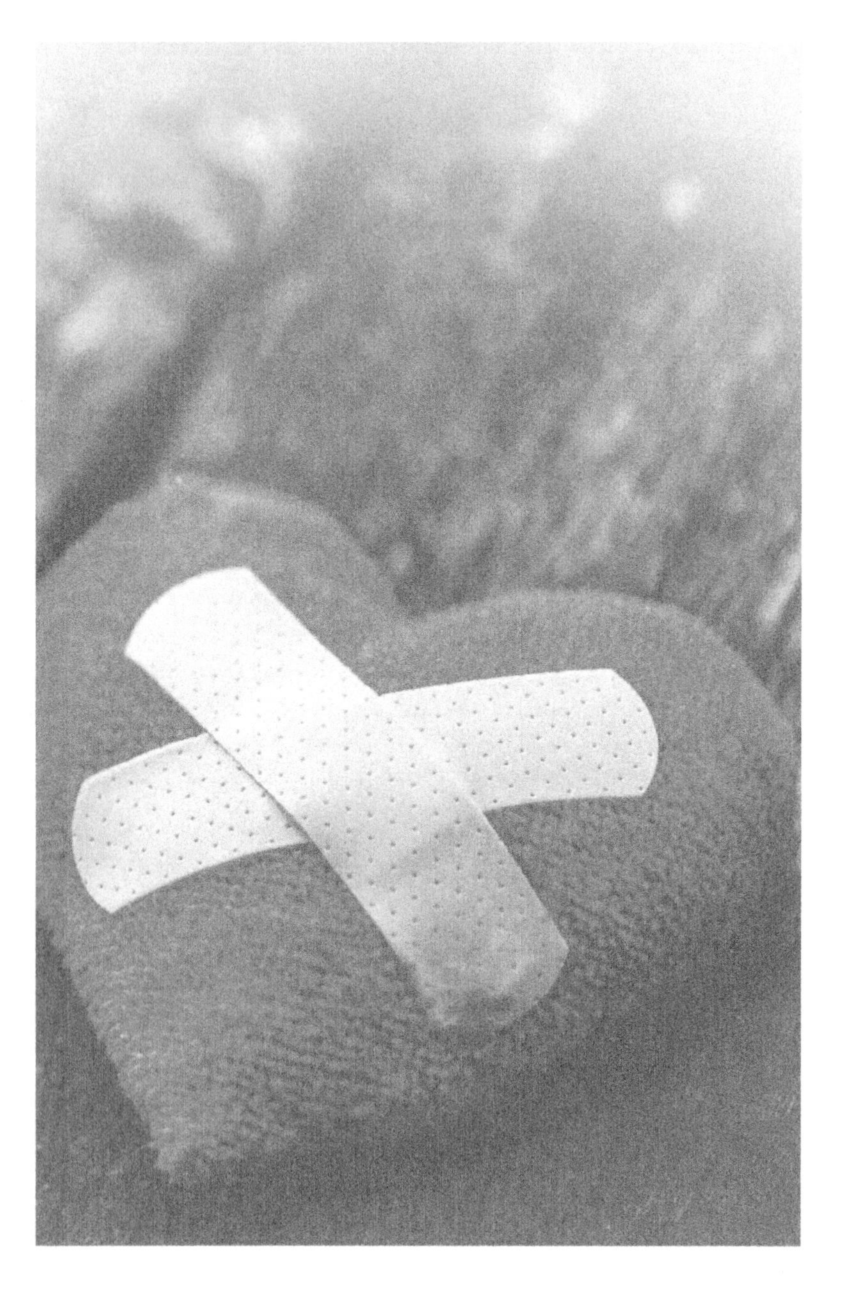

Epilogue

"Have you ever considered you are experiencing so many losses because it's your family's fault?" "I believe it is a spiritual attack on your family because of some unresolved issue."

Let's face it! Many times, when those around us are in a season of grief because of the loss of loved ones, we don't know what to say. It is in times like these we turn to common phrases such as "I know how you feel" or "I can feel your pain." Everyone's painful experience is different. Therefore, you can never take on someone's pain; we all tolerate it differently.

We want to sympathize with others during times of grief, loss, and death, but admittedly, most of us just do not know what to say! Our words and actions are usually well-intentioned, never meaning to cause anyone pain or hurt, but that is exactly the effect they have.

So, what do you say to someone who is grieving? How can your words help with the healing process? In my next book, *When Silence is Golden*, I will seek to cover those awkward moments when a statement that was meant out of love felt like a stinger instead. I will show you how to present gentler and more thoughtful ways to speak and support others through grief.

Acknowledgments

Latisha Sealys, my daughter, thank you for enduring my roller coaster of emotions, putting up with my mood swings, and being my greatest cheerleader and motivator. Also, thank you for encouraging me to take the time to write while you cook and clean.

Rafati Eugene, thank you for always being my rock and support during my period of grief and loss. You put my needs first and provided me with physical and emotional support. Nothing was too much to ask of you. I love the way you embrace my family as your own and, even in my absence, you are my eyes and heart to my family. You encourage me to follow my dream and for that, I am forever thankful.

Merlia Sealys, thank you, my beloved sister, for stepping up to the challenge and keeping the family together in my absence. Thank you, for being there for our siblings, nieces, and nephew. You are a gem, and I am proud of how selfless you have become despite the pressure you face to keep the family together in unity.

Dr. Nadine Collins, a treasure, mentor, coach, spiritual guide, and friend! Thank you for seeing the gold in me, for seeing the vision before I did, for giving me that constant push, for holding my hand as we walk into the labor room of grief. Your investment in me is not taken lightly.

Family and friends, thank you for standing by me and encouraging me along the way. Thanks to those who continue to pray with me and play an important role in my healing process.

And finally, dear reader, thank you for reading *Letting the Pain Out: Learning to Release from Grief and Loss.* I pray the words will not only touch your heart but become the keys used to help release you from the pain of grief and loss. May they encourage you to keep on navigating life and pursuing purpose while grieving your loss.

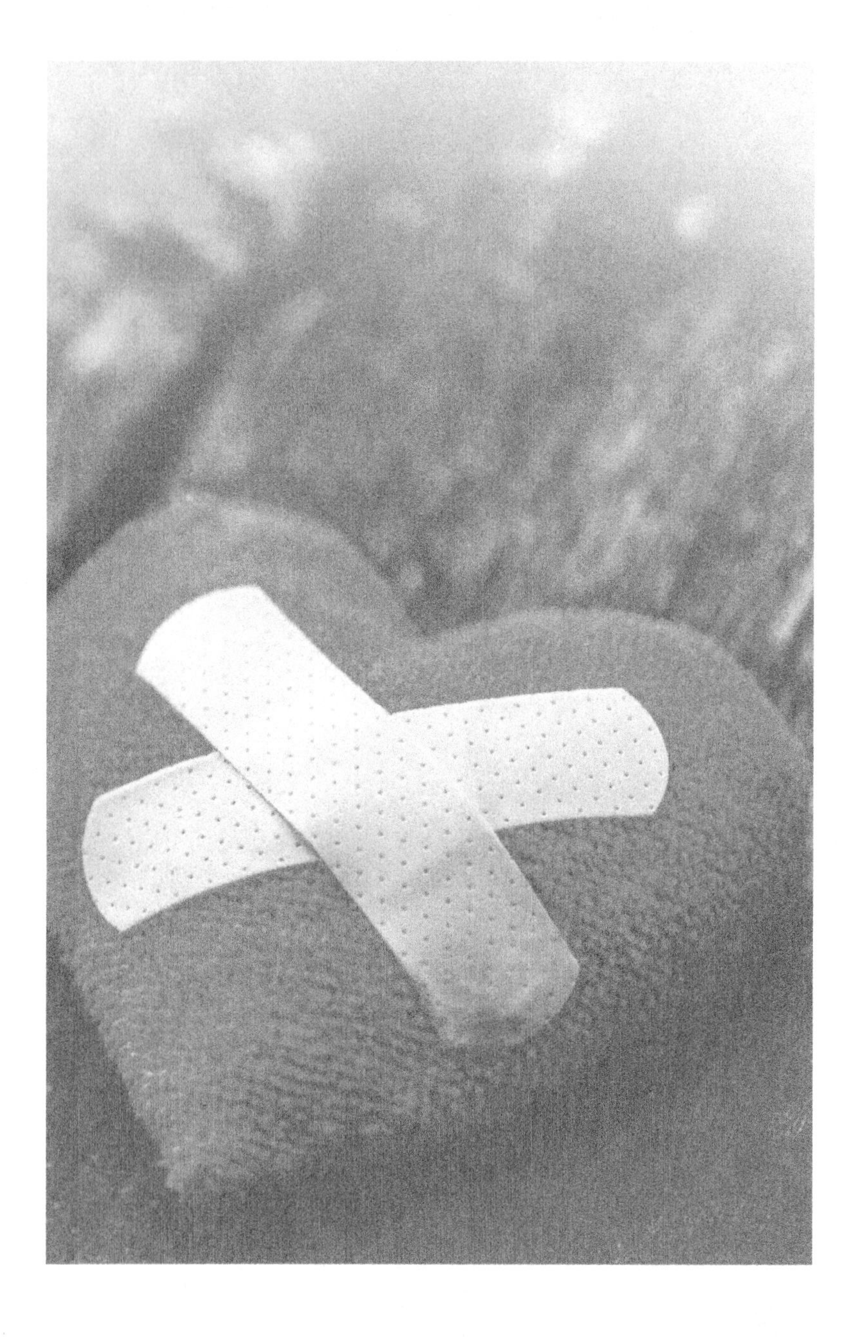

About the Author

Jermila Sealys holds a Bachelor of Science in Nursing with ten years of experience working in the field of Nursing. She is a British Army veteran who went on a mission to Iraq. Her familiarity with sudden death results from the casualties seen on her job and having a significant number of close family members die suddenly.

For six years, she had to deal with the sudden death of loved ones within proximity. After years of bottling up all her emotions and pain, she mustered the courage to release the pain, grief, and loss. She is ready to empower others to step out of the shadows of grief, pain, tears, fears, and guilt to live everyday lives.

Jermila is passionate about working with women who have unexpectedly suffered the loss of loved ones. She is now a Grief Support Coach, Speaker, and Author through her transformation. Her goal is to provide support, empowerment, and education for women to be able to deal with death as a natural part of life and not as seen through taboo lenses.

Printed in Great Britain
by Amazon

12899953R00108